BREAKING OUT OF THE NIMBY MATRIX

Red Pill Success in a Digital NIMBY World

PATRICK SLEVIN

#1 Amazon Bestselling Author of Never Lose to NIMBY Opposition Again!

Printed in the United States of America

First Printing, 2023

Academy of Citizen Engagement

TALLAHASSEE, FL 32311

www.AceMyAudience.com

TABLE OF CONTENTS

FORWARD

The truth about Not-In-My-Backyard (NIMBY) hasn't been thoroughly examined or understood for decades. NIMBY-led controversy is well known to every serious real estate development professional, but oddly, little to nothing has been done to reduce the risks of NIMBYism. NIMBYism costs our economy trillions of dollars in annual losses, yet it goes unmentioned, unexamined, and unchecked for decades.

It begs the question, why?

Every day, NIMBYism lurks in the shadows waiting to attack when developers least expect it. As a third-generation real estate developer, the time has come to change conventional thinking finally, and two-time Amazon bestselling author, former Florida Mayor, and public affairs consultant Patrick Slevin is the man who can help our industry accomplish this endeavor.

In Patrick Slevin's new book, Breaking Out of the NIMBY Matrix™: Red Pill Successes in a Digital NIMBY World, he exposes the shadowy underworld of NIMBYism, detailing where it gets its power, who is behind it, why it happens, and what real estate development professionals must do to be more successful in what he calls the NIMBY Matrix™.

Slevin has written an instant classic, which will become required reading for any serious practitioner in the real estate development industry. His NIMBY Matrix™ framework is an ingenious guide to helping readers see that there's more to NIMBYism than meets the eye.

Those who dare to choose the "red pill" offered by Slevin will be taken down the rabbit hole that will forever change how they perceive NIMBYism. This change in mindset will give readers a competitive advantage. The journey into the NIMBY Matrix™ begins with questioning the sanity of conventional thinking vis-à-vis the go-to "flying under the radar" strategy.

The true secret and genius of Slevin in exposing the NIMBY Matrix™ that's been hiding in plain sight, empowering your opponents, including your competitors. As you go down the rabbit hole with Slevin, you'll quickly realize that NIMBYism cannot be taken at face value – there's more to NIMBYism than we've been led to believe.

In today's Digital Age, it's getting harder to distinguish reality from virtual reality. We're finding NIMBY opposition well adapted in launching their digital activism by using Facebook, websites, blogs, videos, and various apps. Slevin is right when he says developers are abdicating the political high ground to NIMBY forces by "flying under the radar" and giving anti-development opponents the advantage in the traditional and virtual public squares.

Patrick Slevin has creatively illustrated the day-to-day illusions and deceptions that have given the NIMBY Matrix™ its power. No doubt, some status quo agents won't appreciate the realities of NIMBYism being brought out into the light of day.

I've known Patrick for many years, and I've watched him consistently offer information, strategies, and tips to help our industry. Breaking Out of the NIMBY Matrix™: Red Pill Successes in a Digital NIMBY World is a breakthrough roadmap helping readers and industry leaders reduce the risks of NIMBYism. More importantly, it helps those who take the red pill to engage positively and confidently with the community that grants the license to operate.

I'm happy to endorse Slevin's effort and be a part of this long-overdue change.

The success of his book is truly the success of our industry. The more who read it and follow its citizen engagement best practices, the better results we shall see in our professional paths and, more importantly, our real estate development industries.

The only question remains – will you choose the red pill?

Pat Moore
Real Estate Developer
Raleigh, North Carolina

PART I

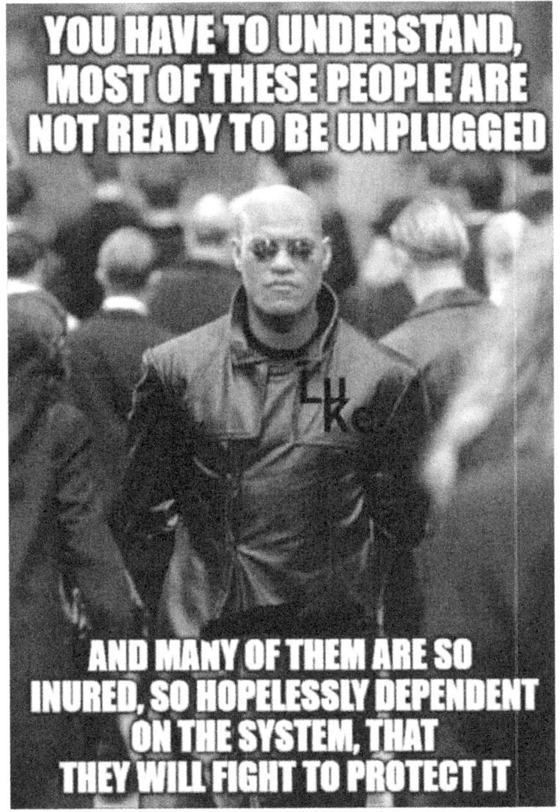

Photo from Movie *The Matrix*

Meme by: Lu Kei

CHOOSE THE RED PILL

Over the last 20 years, a scant number of books have been published on the Not-In-My-Backyard (NIMBY) subject matter. These books were written to help developers after a NIMBY crisis had hit the fan. Unfortunately, these publications were self-promoting ventures, poorly written, too vague, or they simply reiterated dated crisis and grassroots tactics that many practitioners already possessed in their toolboxes. Therefore, they did little to contribute to the communications and citizen engagement best practices over the last several decades.

That is why, February of 2021, I wrote Never Lose to NIMBY Opposition Again!: Master the Secrets, Strategies, and Solutions to Turn NIMBY Crisis Into Your Finest Hour, which became a #1 Amazon bestselling book. It was the first book in decades to provide crisis management best practices for the Digital Age. In less than 90 minutes of reading it, executives, developers, and land-use professionals gained real-time tools to successfully turn high-profile NIMBY threats into project victories regardless of industry, location, and demographics.

In 2021, I gave the development industry a playbook, a "break glass in case of emergency" in the event of a NIMBY crisis. However, there's a better pathway to mitigating and neutralizing NIMBY resistance that's much more profitable, predictable, and practical, but it takes you down the road less traveled.

In my new book, Breaking Out of the NIMBY Matrix™: Red Pill Successes in a Digital NIMBY World, I've focused on helping readers to be more successful in preventing, pre-empting, and prevailing against NIMBY forces. Thanks to the advent of the Digital Age, it's not a question *if* local opposition manifests against you, but *when, where* and *how* does it manifest itself against your development interests.

The public square has become much more virtual. In order to consistently overcome new and improved NIMBY factions, we must be willing to adopt a new perspective.

This new perspective begins by adopting a "red pill" mindset to put yourself in a stronger position to pre-empt and minimize the "shock and awe" tactics that we've come to expect from the opposition. We begin this process by asking a simple question, a question underwriting this book, "Why wait for the opposition to manifest a crisis before taking action?"

TWO NIMBY REALITIES

In Breaking Out of the NIMBY Matrix™: Red Pill Successes in a Digital NIMBY World, I'm going to address the deceptions and denials that have been keeping the real estate development industry in the dark for years. These illusions have exposed good local projects to attacks, while empowering a small, but growing number of anti-development opponents who are responsible for defeating and disrupting an untold number of projects every year, everywhere, in every industry.

I've mentioned a new mindset because there are two realities that define the NIMBY world that we live in: There's the widely accepted illusionary universe where we commonly see NIMBY opposition operating unchallenged, mobilizing their attacks from the digital space, while creating conflicts leading to the defeat of sustainable projects at the municipal level.

Then there's a lesser-known world of modern-day communications and citizen engagement of *Integrated Public Affairs* (IPA) best practices that's mostly seen in the periphery. Over the course of this book, I'll bring this lesser-known reality into the light of day.

In order to bring this lesser known, but emerging world into full view, real estate development leaders and practitioners need to accept the reality that the age-old industry standard of "flying under the radar" is a fading, if not a failing strategy. Make no mistake about it that we've entered a new reality of opposition that I've termed *digital-NIMBY activism*, which exploits the "flying under the radar" practices within the digital realities such as Facebook.

In this virtual world, the opponents evolve into celebrity-type avatars effectively heightening the intensity of attacks against projects. If this virtual reality continues to go unnoticed or ignored by industry practitioners, then it not only increases the risks for more project defeats for you, but also other applicants. In fact, it's been happening for years.

THE BLUE PILL

Over the last few decades NIMBY opponents have leveled up their attacks with digital media channels including Facebook, websites, apps, emails, and blogs. Conversely, over that same span of time, the real estate development industries have remained mostly the same; holding on to their "flying under the radar" atrophy. This status quo mindset has been enabled by the archaic notice and hearing system, as well as other factors that we'll get into.

The notice and hearing process is a legal, logical, and linear construct that has fallen behind the times making it antiquated. Nearly everyone agrees that this system is inept when it comes to educating third-party stakeholders (citizen engagement) – let alone securing the political capital necessary to affect a majority vote approving projects.

I would take it further and argue that the notice and hearing process creates more confusion and conflicts than it does building consensus. In reality, NIMBY factions have not only thrived under this rigid construct, but have become adept at exploiting it, often to the applicant's detriment.

We'll explore more about how developers have conceded to NIMBY factions in *The NIMBY Trifecta* chapter. The result is the opposition consistently trumping permits, site plans, and zoning applications. How do they, a relatively small group of anti-development actors win so often, so easily? When you pull back the curtain, you'll see opponents manufacturing a political, emotional, and chaos-causing construct that's much more persuasive; defeating applicants who blindly adhere to notice and hearing pitfalls.

This adherence to the notice and hearing process is what I consider a blue bill perspective that keeps development industries and professionals in the dark, which in turn enables NIMBYism. The blue pill reference comes from the 1999 blockbuster movie *The Matrix* where the protagonist Mr. Anderson a.k.a. Neo (played by Keanu Reeves) questions the reality around him.

At the beginning of the movie, we find Mr. Anderson, a computer programmer, questioning the nature of reality. He has a nagging feeling that something isn't quite right. He meets with an "international terrorist" known as Morpheus (played by Laurence Fishburne) who offers him a choice between taking a blue or red pill, which will answer his questions about the "real world."

In the context of the movie, taking the red pill means Mr. Anderson will have his eyes opened, enabling him to discover that he's essentially a slave to a dream world manufactured by machines. If Mr. Anderson decides to take the blue pill, then he will continue his life in an illusionary reality manufactured by the machines.

In the context of this book, you can choose to take the blue pill and continue to believe the notice and hearing construct will do the heavy lifting of educating third-party stakeholders. You can press forward with the "flying under the radar" strategy, believing that it's the safest way to protect and promote your development priorities.

Or you can choose the red pill where we found Morpheus enticing Mr. Anderson by saying, "You take the blue pill...the story ends, you wake up in your bed and believe whatever you want to believe. You take the red pill...you stay in Wonderland, and I show you how deep the rabbit hole goes."

THE RED PILL

So, I'm offering you a choice. You can take the metaphoric blue bill, put this book down, go back to your day-to-day ways where you can continue to "fly under the radar," and hope the notice and hearing construct withstands the onslaught of NIMBY conflicts. Unfortunately, there will be a number of folks who will choose the blue pill way, pretending this book doesn't exist, or they'll disparage me as "international terrorist" peddling red pills so they can protect their status quo interests. In either case, the "devil you know" mindset is very strong and creates fear even in the hearts and minds of the greatest of risk takers.

Or you can break out of the prison of conventional thinking by taking the metaphoric red pill to go deep down the rabbit hole. I promise you, the change of mindset will empower you to confidently operate and succeed at higher levels of success in this digital NIMBY world.

THE BOOK

Perception is reality when it comes to interpreting the world around us. Unfortunately, the false realities of the NIMBY Matrix™ have been sustained by blue bill conventional thinking for too long. The strategies, tactics, best practices, and secrets that I share in this book can only be realized by professionals who are willing to question the wisdom of conventional thinking.

There are two parts to this book. In Part I, I'll break down the conventional thinking and the gatekeepers or agents who have kept corporate executives, developers, and land-use professionals in a dream-like state of mind. I will then profile the rise of the next generation of anti-development opponents that mobilize under *The Rise of the NIMBY Avatars* chapter. In that chapter, we'll jump into the virtual world of digital-NIMBY activism and how opponents successfully demonize and defeat projects within the constructs of the digital world.

In Part II of the book, we'll pivot with our new perspective and apply it to *Integrated Public Affairs* (IPA) practices. In today's digital world, applicants need more than a public relations operative, political consultant, or marketing pro to effectively neutralize digital NIMBYism. In fact, you will need all of these disciplines and more. I will break down the respective disciplines of communications and citizen

engagement that are easily and effortlessly integrated under the public affairs umbrella.

THE POWER OF PUBLIC AFFAIRS

I'm a public affairs generalist who has excelled in many specialties including crisis management, issues advocacy, public relations, corporate communications, political marketing, coalition building, media relations, and grassroots advocacy. However, there are specialties that I know just enough that I need to bring in or collaborate with experts in their respective specialties of videography, digital media, and land-use law. Many corporate developers and organizations have these specialists on the payroll or locally contracted, but they're either separated by corporate silos or excluded from the real estate development approval process.

Integrated public affairs is a team approach that effectively reconciles the complexities often found in multiple disciplines of communications and advocacy. For example, you often find corporate communications, which is focused on engaging shareholders, industry media, employees et.al. Alternatively, public affairs is focused on influencing political stakeholders who determine public policy at the federal, state, and municipal levels.

These two communication disciplines have their own lexicon that's driven by corporate subcultures and their respective silos. I've counseled clients on both sides of these disciplines, acting in many cases as a literal translator. I'll identify and break down these silos to give you a corporate roadmap toward success.

In Part II, I've invited experts in their respective fields to contribute as co-chapter contributors to the chapters of videography, digital media, and legal. These contributors are part of my cadre of experts with whom I've collaborated to effectively neutralize local opposition over the years. I appreciate that they've agreed to share their time and talent for the benefit of the book and you.

WHY INTEGRATED PUBLIC AFFAIRS?

The challenge for any development application is transforming it from two-dimensional site plans, blueprints, and structures into a human narrative. This is important because presenting a human narrative requires a third-dimensional campaign: A delivery of emotional impressions that influence the perceptions of public officials and local stakeholders.

Integrated public affairs achieves both the strategic and tactical necessities to give you the better best practices to humanize your projects, which is necessary to neutralize and defeat today's digital NIMBY opponents. I will share my simple equation that powers any successful integrated public affairs campaign.

In my 25+ years of engaging NIMBY opposition, I've found that every project has the ability to reduce the risks and overcome the NIMBY odds, when implementing the public affairs tools outlined in Part II.

Moreover, a pre-empting mindset is much more preferable than reacting to crisis. Even though I didn't realize it in my earlier years, part of my success was finding the integrated public affairs solutions, which frankly were hiding in plain sight.

In short, I have successfully traversed the corporate silos and blue pill obstacles that are currently empowered by the conventional thinking paradigm. The good news for you is many of the strategies and solutions to neutralizing NIMBYism and reducing the risks of political rejection, already exist within your world. It's just a matter of being able to perceive that world through a slightly different lens, which this book will help you acquire.

Here's a glass of water and the red pill. Let's see where the rabbit hole takes us.

TRUST IN THE TRENCHES

Congratulations! You decided to take the red pill. You've chosen an adventure to not only go down the rabbit hole, but venture on the road less traveled. It's a big deal!

For many, this is not an easy journey, nor should it be. The "flying under radar" approach is a powerful mindset because it's reliable, familiar, and safe. I'm the first to recognize that it has merit and not completely futile. I work closely with clients who want to go slow and incremental to overcome their low-risk tolerances. I completely understand changing business practices, models, and even cultures require a series of successes to gain compliance before strategies can be fully implemented.

When you embark on changing a paradigm there's an inherent fear of failure. No one wants to fail. Failing is an awful feeling. This is where risk aversion keeps many of us from progressing forward vis-à-vis keeping the status quo in place.

In my experience "flying under the radar" creates more risks of failure than it does of increasing the odds for success. Let me give you an example of how keeping a low profile feeds a negative feedback loop trapping developers in a deceptive blue pill construct.

NEGATIVE FEEDBACK LOOP

Over 90 percent of the negative news stories reported on projects originate from the opposition. Why is that?

The developer's "flying under the radar" attitude is governed by the question, "Why unnecessarily draw attention to ourselves, creating problems, if there isn't any opposition in sight?". There's logic behind that thinking, but it's flawed. On the surface, it's easy to see the vast majority of news stories on development are negative, which gives the opposition the ability to fan the flames of controversy. So, under this lens, the news media is hardly seen as approachable, let alone fair in their reporting. But there's another side to the story that you don't hear about.

Reporters are sketch artists and not painters. Meaning, they don't have deep knowledge about real estate development or anything about your projects or applications, so when they get pitched by the opposition, their viewpoints are slanted against the project. The reporter's first impression is negatively framed, and now she has a juicy story with conflict built in, and the developer is cast as the stereotypical antagonist. It's a formula for success in the reporter's mind, which is very difficult to change once it takes a life of its own.

To complete the story, the reporter finally calls the developer late in the afternoon asking for a quote with the deadline imminent. In most scenarios, the story was already written before the developer gets called. The drafted story is ready to go to the editor with negative quotes from the NIMBY opposition and more often than not, comments from public officials expressing their concerns. The reporter just needs a token quote from the developer to close out the story.

BAM! Negative publicity is born with the developer's quote buried towards the bottom third of the article, which no one will see. So, who is responsible for this negative reporting? In order to answer that, let's ask a series of questions that will help lead to an answer that you may not have thought about:

- Is it really the reporter's fault?
- Could the story have been told differently had the developer proactively contacted the reporter instead of the opposition?
- Would the reporter have benefitted from being directed to a project website or emailed a Questions & Answers document breaking down the project in laymen's terms?
- Would the story have been more balanced, even favorable, had the developer offered the reporter the contact info to local allies/influencers who'll speak in favor of the project to counter the local opposition?

Conventional thinking argues against reaching out to the reporter or having elements in place to engage the media. Conventional thinking considers proactive or responsive posturing as too risky or reckless, so developers become sitting ducks waiting to be shot out of the water. But I'm getting ahead of myself.

The above scenario demonstrates how developers passively help facilitate negative feedback loops manifesting negative publicity. They strategically decide to keep their heads low, allowing the opposition to make the first move. As a result, the reporter has an "evil developer" frame-of-mind, while interviewing elected officials, getting them anxious, then the negative news article gets published, where we find the developer shaking his head blaming the news media for not being fair or balanced.

This loop has repeated itself every day of every month of every year for decades. Yet, the status quo prevails, falsely affirming the "flying under the radar" paradigm. Thus, the loop keeps on playing like a broken record.

Of course, not every project experiences NIMBY opposition nor do projects get voted down after being negatively profiled in the news media. I would argue this has become more the exception than the rule. Maybe 20-30 years ago this model would win more often than not, but in today's Digital Age its more akin to rolling the dice.

TRUST IN THE TRENCHES

I don't expect you to agree with everything I've laid out in my book. If I'm able to empower you to evaluate your practices, identify areas for improvement, breached some silos, and plug in some elements of integrated public affairs, then my book did its job.

However, I'm not satisfied with that outcome. If you're going down the rabbit hole, then you deserve my best efforts to empower you. In order to achieve that, I must earn your trust. When I'm brought onto a new project there's a certain level of trust extended between me and my clients. It's a two-way street and I call it "Trust in the Trenches."

The best way to earn your trust is to share one of my greatest professional failures as a consultant. I failed to convince the client to follow a key recommendation that proved to be very costly to both of us. I knew if he didn't follow my counsel that it would be detrimental to not just his interests, but the entire state of Florida.

I'm sharing this failure for three reasons. One: I had my share of failures. Two, I don't trust anyone who says they've never failed. Success is borne out of failure. Three, if we're going the way of the red pill, then I want to keep it real by sharing how I've learned from one of my biggest failures. If I can gain your trust and credibility, then it's worth reliving this tale for your benefit.

GO NEGATIVE OR RISK FAILURE

Back in the mid 2000's Florida was experiencing a new form of NIMBYism via ballot-box initiatives. Citizens who didn't want a new development or rezoning to be approved, they would gather signatures via a petition to place the project on the local municipal ballot. Thus, usurping the vote of local elected officials. This didn't happen by accident.

The emergence of this ballot-box NIMBYism was championed by operatives who founded an anti-development group called Florida Hometown Democracy.

By 2006, they scored a few minor victories in local municipalities, but they weren't considered a real threat. However, that would change in 2006 at the beach town of St. Pete Beach located on the gulf side of the Tampa Bay area. In St. Pete Beach, Florida Hometown Democracy operatives worked closely with local proxies to forge a petition drive to restrict the hoteliers from renovating their buildings, especially with height restrictions.

Due to the eight hurricanes Florida experienced in 2004 and 2005, FEMA put into place new boundaries for shoreline development. This affected the hotel operators who sought renovations and rebuilding. Suffice it to say, opposition didn't want their oceanic views obscured by increased height, so a local opposition group formed and gathered the requisite signatures.

Of course, the hoteliers fought the petition initiative in court. And of course, they lost in court. That's when I was brought on to put together a political campaign to defeat five anti-development ballot measures. The catch was timing. When the court made its ruling, I had less than two weeks to organize a full-throttle campaign before the start of absentee voting, which was to begin in just 10 days!

We were very late to the party. The opposition had over a year of attacking hotel development with no organized responses coming from the local hotel community. The hoteliers truly believed their lawyers who told them they would successfully defeat the measures in court, so they never were concerned with winning votes at the ballot box.

Within a few days of coming on board, I brought in two local campaign consultants, one republican, one democrat who often campaigned against each other, we formed a political action committee (PAC), organized a grassroots coalition comprised of hoteliers, vendors, and community leaders, and finally we launched an aggressive direct mail campaign. The first direct mail piece arrived on the same day as absentee ballots.

The opposition was well organized and intense. Florida Hometown Democracy needed to win this municipal battle to establish their ballot box model to roll out across the state. As it would turn out, St. Pete Beach become ground zero in the battle to defeat Florida Hometown Democracy. Alas, no one in Tallahassee gave much notice or concern despite my waving the red flags. I had one development trade association contribute $1000 to our PAC, but the rest of the $300,000+ would be raised locally, which was quite a feat.

In a few weeks, we had our campaign humming. We put the opposition on the defensive, taking them off message, our coalition was strong with very influential surrogates. We had the local mayor endorsing our cause. Yet, there was one thing we still needed to do. The opposition, these out-of-towners, weren't being attacked by us, or by anyone. This was a problem.

As the campaign manager and lead consultant, I arranged the meeting with my two campaign consultants to discuss strategy with the client. Both of my political consultants were lobbying hard for the campaign to attack the opposition with direct mail before absentee voting ended.

The meeting didn't go well. Despite our best counsel, the client (one of the major hotel resorts) refused to endorse anything that would be perceived as negative. My two consultants, both with over 20 years of political campaign experience, looked at me and shook their heads in dismay.

I advised the client that this decision could cost us a victory. He stuck to his guns asserting, "We still have to coexist with our neighbors, and I don't want to create an unnecessary divide in the community...you don't live here, but we do." It was clear that the conversation was getting personal for the client, so I backed down and accepted my orders of nothing negative.

Leaving the meeting, I failed both my team and my client. This was a crucial campaign tactic that would ensure we defeated a savvy opponent.

On Election Day, we were feeling great about the exit polling and votes that were being tallied. Our track polling over the last 10 days showed a daily increase of support for our positions. At the Election Day watch party, the initial wave of votes came in and we had convincedly won the vote count on Election Day. The track polling was accurate. We were cautiously optimistic, but we still were waiting on the absentee vote count, which hadn't come in yet.

The absentee votes came in. We weren't surprised that we lost the absentee votes by a troubling margin. Now it would come down to how much of a buffer our Election Day votes would offset the absentee votes. Could we withstand the consequences of starting our campaign 10 days before voting began, when no one even knew us or our arguments for voting against the measures? We won on Election Day, because we had over a month to reach and inform voters, but during the absentee period, we were mostly unknown to the voters.

When all the votes were finally tallied, we defeated the first four measures, which were less controversial. The issue of height was the main prize for both camps.

We lost the height measure by a total of 21 votes!

No doubt the decision not to attack the opposition, going negative, came back to bite us in the ass.

I'll never forget the look on the client's face when he read the reports. He looked up, shocked, and pained asking in a strained voice, "How did this happen?" I said to him that we condensed a six-month political campaign into six-week blitzkrieg, and we won on Election Day and lost the absentee vote.

I wasn't going to say to him that had we attacked the opposition we would have won. What would that achieve? Yes, he made the final decision, but I failed as a consultant to help him come to the best decision for his interests.

Florida Hometown Democracy capitalized on the victory spreading their ballot-box NIMBYism model across the state, while pushing their statewide ballot initiative. The business lobbying groups in Tallahassee that initially ignored my warnings now took notice. In 2010, after millions of dollars were raised and spent by a business coalition, the Hometown ballot initiative was defeated.

All this could have been avoided had I overcame 21 votes, which would have stopped them in 2006.

Even today, it still sucks reliving my failure for the benefit of sharing it here. Nevertheless, I believed then, as I do now, we could have won had I convinced the client to attack early in the campaign. In retrospect, I should have invited other hoteliers who were coalition partners and peers to weigh in on the decision making, but I hadn't anticipated any issues.

Lesson learned.

FAILING FORWARD TOWARD SUCCESS

In 2007, I had a rematch with Florida Hometown Democracy and their proxies on the east coast of Florida in the City of Edgewater just south of Daytona. This time it was a proposed master-planned community with 3.2 million square feet of commercial that was in the crosshairs of their ballot-box

NIMBYism. I was called in after the courts ruled in favor of placing the anti-development petitions on the ballot.

This time, we had over three months to kill the first of what would become two waves of ballot measures. One measure in particular would add to Edgewater's charter no development beyond "one unit per 20 acres", which would have killed my client's $150 million proposed master-planned community.

Unlike St. Pete Beach, we totally defeated Hometown's anti-development ballot measures. My prior failure in St. Pete Beach was not going to be repeated. The client fully trusted my counsel. Even better, we spent less than $100,000 to defeat a slew of ballot measures over the span of two elections, which was icing on the cake of sweet success.

Our coalition partners attacked the opposition calling out their out-of-town operatives every chance we had. Going negative helped secure victory. We won both early voting and Election Day votes, as well as elected pro-project candidates who approved our requested comp plan amendments during this timeframe.

Victory is only sweet because we've tasted the bitterness of defeat. It's important that we agree that failure is part of the process of achieving success. We cannot have one without the other.

Make no mistake about it, I want you to take this book and be more successful in neutralizing NIMBYism. Don't let failure or the fear of failure stand in your way to greater success.

THE INSANITY OF COVENTIONAL THINKING

"Reality is merely an illusion, albeit a very persistent one."

Albert Einstein

Albert Einstein forever changed how we perceived the world with his theory of relativity over 118 years ago. He single-handedly changed the conventional thinking of Newtonian physics, which influenced western society for centuries positing that we live in an orderly and predictable universe.

That would start to change in 1905, when Einstein turned the world of physics upside down with his theory of relativity. The scientific establishment (conventional thinking of the day) wasn't ready to accept Einstein's revolutionary theories at first. He posed a threat to the very foundation to the nature of reality. Thankfully, after many years of experiments, the establishment finally relented to Einstein's genius and his $E=MC^2$ shifting paradigm.

During that period of fighting the establishment Einstein said, "The world as we have created it is a process of our thinking. It cannot be changed without changing our thinking."

Today, the real estate industries' current thinking, conventional thinking, about NIMBYism is mostly indifferent. This is my observation based on over 25 years of studying, writing, speaking, and counseling in the real estate development world. Think about it. How many academic papers have been published? How many industry surveys have been conducted? How many committees dedicated to resolving NIMBYism in America?

The short answer is little to none. However, there's one study that was shocking and revolutionary at the same time.

PROJECT ~~NO PROJECT~~ STUDY

In 2011, The U.S. Chamber published a mind blowing report titled, *PROJECT NO PROJECT Progress Denied: A Study on Potential Economic Impact of Permitting Challenges Facing Proposed Energy Projects*. The introduction to the report stated:

> "For years, we knew of anecdotal evidence that projects were being delayed or stopped throughout the nation, but there was no study that

> systematically examined the circumstances of such challenged projects.
> To address this information shortfall, Chamber staff implemented
> Project No Project, an initiative that assesses the broad range of energy
> projects that are being stalled, stopped, or outright killed nationwide
> due to "Not In My Back Yard" (NIMBY) activism, a broken permitting process
> and a system that allows limitless challenges by opponents of development."

The Chamber's findings were shocking, but not surprising. They studied 351 energy projects across the country that were impacted by NIMBYism. They revealed the cost of NIMBYism was over $1.1 trillion in economic impact, while killing 1.9 million jobs. The study found "NIMBY activists" were winning more often than losing. They found that the archaic permitting and siting process, coupled with NIMBY activists' adeptness at exploiting this process significantly undermined our economy: "Economic and job impact projections of this study show that millions of jobs, and hundreds of billions of dollars in potential economic value, continue to sit on the shelf."

In their conclusion the report stated, "The Chamber believes that our nation's complex, disorganized regulatory process for siting and permitting new facilities and its frequent

manipulation by NIMBY activists constitute a major impediment to economic development and job creation."

Finally in the report, the Chamber called on others to build upon their findings:

> "This study should be viewed as a first attempt to evaluate the permit challenges. We ask others to add to the body of work being developed and help us better improve our methodology for determining the lost economic and job opportunities that result from a failed permitting process. We encourage economists, think tanks, academics, and other interested parties to not only read the study but provide us feedback that might be helpful in refining our analysis."

Think about it for moment. If only 351 energy projects, that were delayed and defeated by NIMBYism, can cost $1.1 trillion in lost economic value and 1.9 million jobs, then how much more is lost when you factor in other industries in real estate development? How many more trillions of dollars are lost, every year, to NIMBYism targeting master-planned communities, mixed use, multi-family, infill, retail, affordable housing, mining, landfills, sports entertainment, hospitality, resorts, high rises, shopping malls, hospitals, renewable energy, and the list goes on.

The U.S. Chamber exposed a national syndrome constantly threatening our economic vitality back in 2011. The question is how many other economists, think tanks, academics, authors, and other interested parties carried on their groundbreaking research from there?

The answer is ZERO!

TURNING INSANITY TO ENLIGHTENMENT

Going back to Einstein. It was shocking back in the day to understand that we no longer lived in a universe operating like a predictable and orderly clock, but rather a chaotic universe with a space-time continuum that felt more like science fiction than fact.

It's time (pun intended) for the real estate development establishment to embrace a new mindset, a new paradigm of thinking in order to realistically deal with the growing NIMBY syndrome. It begins by acknowledging that conventional thinking is just a much a threat to future development than community opposition.

Einstein helps us here with one of his famous quotes, "Insanity is doing the same thing, over and over again, but expecting different results." In short, the real estate development industries must transcend beyond its rigid and archaic practices to protect projects from NIMBYism at the municipal levels.

As we continue into the book, you'll start to see more and more how conventional thinking gives birth and power to the NIMBY Matrix™. By taking the red pill, you're on your way to changing your thinking. The result is gaining a perspective where you can address the causes of NIMBYism rather than fighting the symptoms.

We're overdue for a paradigm shift that upgrades conventional thinking with more modern-day strategies that personify corporate reputations and good neighbor practices. This enables corporate developers to adopt integrated public affairs in Part II.

There you'll find and learn my equation for integrated public affairs (IPA) to successfully win political and social support for projects:

But first, let's discuss in the next chapter revealing what is the NIMBY Matrix™ and the agents enforcing its status quo, conventional thinking paradigm.

THE ENEMY WITHIN

Welcome to the NIMBY Matrix™! Before I can show you how to break out of it, I must take you down the rabbit hole in this chapter, so you can see its current constructs. As we descend, let's start with the simple premise that NIMBYism is in the eye of the beholder, it's subjective, and open to interpretation.

What you see and what I see is influenced by our education, experiences, and interpretation of the world "out there." Therefore, it's one thing to gain a new perspective on NIMBYism, but it's another to act upon a greater awareness that challenges your thinking and comfort zones.

The Greek Philosopher Plato knew about the dangers of status quo thinking and clinging to the "devil we know" when he said, "We can easily forgive a child who is afraid of the dark; the real tragedy of this life is when men are afraid of the light."

The NIMBY Matrix™ has successfully kept the real estate development industries in the dark for nearly a half a century. As a result, the NIMBY phenomena has become stronger, more dangerous, and costlier every year. In order to see the realities of the NIMBY Matrix™, you must be openminded and prepared to be challenged mentally and emotionally. Let's see where the rabbit hole takes us.

THE NIMBY MATRIX™

Every time a corporate developer or land-use professional decides to "fly under the radar," they're consciously *avoiding* or *ignoring* the risks of local opposition. This is the epitome of conventional thinking that defaults to rolling the dice with millions, if not billions of dollars at stake.

The NIMBY Matrix™ derives its energy and existence from this conventional mindset. When someone utters the words or even thinks "let's fly under the radar," it acts much like an "Open Sesame" secret passcode opening the entrance to a fabled cave of thieves. But in this case, "fly under the radar" manifests the NIMBY Matrix™.

In other words, the NIMBY Matrix™ is constructed by professional indifference to it and energized by the fear of changing the conventional thinking that is firmly in place. It is psychological in its constructs as well as the perception of the realities we live in each and every day.

So, what I'm getting at is this --- the NIMBY Matrix™ begins with you!

Whether or not you're aware of how it has deceived you with its false constructs is a question only you can answer.

However, like Neo, our hero in *The Matrix* movie, something drove you, cued you to take the red pill by reading this book.

EMBRACE YOUR SHADOW

Psychologist Carl Jung wrote of the willful blindness of the majority of human beings to what he called our "shadow"... that counterfeit portion of ourselves that we stuff into the unconscious, so we don't have to deal with it.

"One does not become enlightened by imagining figures of light but by making the darkness conscious. The latter procedure, however, is disagreeable and therefore not popular," said Jung.

Now you may be realizing that when I offered to take you down the rabbit hole, I'm in fact taking you deeper within yourself. The undisclosed secret to the NIMBY Matrix™ is found within each of us. When it's unexamined, it's truly an enemy within; acting like a shadow that we don't want to recognize or engage.

We must be willing to exorcise it away with self-revelation, self-awareness, and courage, but that's just the start. There are forces that don't want you to embrace your shadow of conventional thinking nor break out of the NIMBY Matrix™.

BEWARE THE NIMBY MATRIX™ AGENTS

As we discussed earlier, *The Matrix* is run by machines, but more disturbing is the machines protect themselves with agents such as the Mr. Smith character whose mission is to enforce the false reality that keeps humanity in its dream state. Whenever someone gets unplugged with a red pill, Mr. Smith and his fellow agents, are dispatched to suppress revolts that may destabilize the deceptive system.

Every industry in real estate development has its own agents enforcing the NIMBY Matrix™ that we encounter today. They do an excellent job keeping the status quo in place by enabling and encouraging a "flying under the radar" mindset that conform to conventional thinking.

These NIMBY Matrix™ agents can be anywhere and anyone. They could very well be your colleagues, partners, editors, professors, association executives, authors, communicators, and certainly competitors.

Think about it: Every year there are hundreds of national conventions, conferences, and local chapter meetings. You can count on both hands and feet the number of programs that spend 45-60 minutes discussing the topic of NIMBY. If asked why they don't offer more in-depth programs on NIMBYism, the predictable answer is it's not what members want. The follow up question would be, "which members?"

At best, these programs offered recalibrated tactics and retreaded messaging that remain within the parameters of conventional thinking i.e. reactive, passive, and inept = innocuous.

WHO ARE THE AGENTS?

Who are the agents enforcing the NIMBY Matrix™...and what is the evidence of their existence?

It's very clear that professional real estate organizations and the leaders behind them don't want you to acknowledge or even know about the growing threat posed by the NIMBY phenomena.

This is evidenced by the absence of serious study, discussion, and development of new practices, which continues to protect conventional Newtonian thinking in our digital NIMBY world.

Back to the U.S. Chamber's *Project No Project* study on NIMBY. It was met with a collective thud of silence. It has been ignored despite the researchers' call for other industries to expand upon the shocking data collected. Their calls went ignored, and the status quo wheels kept on turning.

These NIMBY Matrix™ agents are exceptionally good. They exist at every level from local offices and local trade chapters to corporate board rooms and trade association leadership. The majority find safety and security by looking away from the light and accepting the shadows of truth: periodically sponsoring a "lunch and learn" type forum on the topic, which is better than nothing, but focused only on addressing the symptoms not the true origins of the problem.

Then there is a small, but powerful number of nefarious agents who are adept at manipulating our perceptions from the shadows. These agents have their hands on the levers of influence in the board rooms, editorial suites, and trade boards deciding what their respective development industries say and don't say about NIMBYism. The collective indifference is found in their silence, which can be deafening.

I've seen firsthand how these agents operate. It's not easy to spot them, but the few glimpses you catch are proof enough. In order to spot them, you must answer the question, "Who benefits most when my projects are defeated by NIMBYism?"

The answer will lead you to your competitors. It's the real estate development industry's dirtiest secret. There are competitors in many different industries who not only covertly instigate local opposition against fellow developers, but also suppress best practices from reaching you through respective trade organizations and their publications. Let me say, not every trade association is in on the fix, but there's enough of them to keep the NIMBY Matrix™ humming.

Why do they do this? The answer is simple – to protect their market share and their positions in the industry.

The big box wars in the early 2000s is one of many examples of proof. When a Super Walmart was looking to get approved at the local level, we'd see NIMBY opposition rise up. However, the vast majority of those uprisings were sponsored behind the scenes by labor unions, grocery competitors, and other big box competitors. These competitors hired savvy national public affairs firms to covertly manufacture what we call "Astroturf campaigns" against Walmart and countless other unsuspecting applicants.

This is happening even to this day. Therefore, you cannot afford to accept NIMBY opposition at face value. They're not always affluent homeowners fearing just change, but willing proxies operating on behalf of your competitors. You'd be surprised how often these agents are pulling the strings outside of your perception.

Make no mistake about it, these NIMBY Matrix™ agents are the gatekeepers preventing you from acquiring greater awareness, which prevents you from breaking away from an aging paradigm of thought and practice.

FORBIDDEN KNOWLEDGE

With knowledge does come power. But understand that any attempt to disrupt the establishment is often met with resistance, which I've endured and overcome for years. Certainly, the book that you're reading now will be seen as a direct threat to the establishment. It will be either discredited or ignored.

However, this hasn't stopped me from getting my red pill successes out to high-achieving clients who want to win. Despite being shut out of national conferences and conventions, I've been successful in covertly flying under the NIMBY Matrix's radar, fighting the good fight for my clients across the country.

The question for you: Will you continue to conform to the prevailing paradigm of conventional thinking when it comes to overcoming NIMBYism, or will you take on the NIMBY Matrix™ and break out of its clutches?

You've acquired some forbidden knowledge, but do you have the courage to act on it? I hope you do. This is a hard decision for most people, because changing one's perspective isn't always easy, especially when the status quo is primed to suppress nonconforming voices.

If you remain skeptical, I'd say that's fair at this stage of the book. I have no doubt there will be agents criticizing my book as conspiracy theory or written by a self-serving hack looking to sell books. Such barbs don't concern me, because I write and operate from a solid foundation of knowledge, character, and record of success.

What I can promise you by reading this book is that it will free you from the fetters of the establishment's conventional thinking.

If anyone, especially the agents, challenge you about breaking of the NIMBY Matrix™, simply ask them this rhetorical question, "Over the last 5 to 10 years, how much has NIMBY opposition affected your bottom line or the bottom line interests of your members?" I'm willing to bet that most won't know the answer, or they can only guess at the figure.

That's because no one wants to quantify or even qualify the monetary impact when we are defeated by NIMBY opposition. It is painful to face the shadow of something too unpopular to acknowledge and confront.

So, I encourage you not to give in to the enemy within you (the status quo mindset) and the agents protecting their conventional-thinking industry. They don't and never have had your best interests at heart.

THE NIMBY TRIFECTA

Let me be direct and to the point: The opposition wants to destroy your credibility. Credibility is your greatest political currency, and they know it. To defeat you, they must discredit you. This is done by instigating conflict that leads to crisis, which in turn, influences public officials to vote against real estate development projects and applications – especially during election years.

Conflict is the conduit to destroying your credibility. Conflict disrupts the civility of public discourse, which is their X-Factor. If you can overcome this X-Factor, then you can begin protecting your projects against these anti-development forces.

But first, you must be able to see how the conflict is manufactured and why good projects get consistently delayed, disrupted, and defeated on nearly a daily basis.

There are three elements the opposition must have in place in order to manifest the conflict threatening good real estate projects. These elements can be likened to starting a fire, which you need the three elements of oxygen, fuel, and a spark. In the case of NIMBY opposition, I call it the NIMBY Trifecta, which is a powerful formula enabling anti-development forces to defeat developers.

The NIMBY Matrix™ is sustained by this NIMBY trifecta, so when you learn about what causes the chaos and conflict, then you can begin venturing down a path to more success and less failure.

Let's take them one at a time.

ELEMENT 1: GOSSIP

When I decided to run for mayor at 26 in 1995, one of the first actions I took was to introduce myself to a group of men, about a dozen, who got together at the local Einstein Bagels every morning. These older gentlemen were opinion leaders who knew all the gossip in our city. They gossiped more than the ladies at the beauty parlor. They knew who was having affairs, who was going bankrupt, and who was up or down in local politics.

If I was going to win my campaign for mayor, I had to at least keep these chatty gentlemen neutral, and hopefully lean towards supporting my efforts to be elected mayor against the entrenched incumbent. Fortunately, they weren't happy with the current mayor and were happy to share their knowledge about him, while endorsing my campaign. Their word-of-mouth was a very powerful tool.

The greatest weapon in the NIMBY arsenal is the grapevine firing off its community gossip. In many cases, the grapevine spreads gossip months *before* the development application is even submitted. In a growing number of cases, by the time the application is officially filed, opponents have already spooked neighbors, developed an anti-project Facebook page, initiated emails, texts, and *Nextdoor* calls to action.

These rumor mills deliver mischaracterizations and lies spanning a wide range of emotionally charged allegations that fan status quo fears. The allegations are predictable and tired, but still effective: The proposed application will increase traffic, decrease property values, increase crime rates, lose jobs, close businesses, pollute (water, noise, light, air) the environment, endanger species, cause radiation, raise taxes, destroy the character of the community, stress our infrastructure, and the list goes on.

A NIMBY grapevine easily spreads gossip with the help of Facebook, whisper campaigns, and bureaucratic notices, which aggregately jacks up fears of change, resentment, and prejudices. Developers typically pick up on some of this gossip and hearsay, but too often don't fully realize the extent of the opposition that's amassing against the project until it's way too late.

Mark Twain had this to say about gossip, "A lie can travel halfway around the world, while the truth is still putting on its shoes." We've all seen how rumors are treated like fires, no one admits to starting them and before you know it, they're out of control.

ELEMENT 2: NOTICE & HEARING PROCESS

For decades, developers and land-use professionals have based their financial projections, business models, and professional practices on a notice and hearing system that's reliably *legal*, *logical*, and *linear*. There's a predictability and stability that has given them a sense of certainty going through the application process.

However, if you've been in the real estate development space for any period of time, then you're no stranger to the archaic mechanisms of the notice and hearing process. Ironically, one of the main reasons for the notice and hearing system was facilitating public participation and encouraging public education. In most cases, it has resulted in the exact opposite.

The unintended consequences of the notice and hearing process have been many. It has substantiated rumors with its bureaucratic notices, it has created perceptions of favoritism to deep-pocketed developers, and it has empowered opponents who are highly adept at exploiting the predictability of the notice and hearing process. What was good in theory, public participation, has never quite played out in practice.

Moreover, the notice and hearing process hasn't effectively executed citizen participation, so applicants have operated with a certain tunnel vision setting them up for NIMBY ambush.

As soon as a project application is formally submitted for review before a local planning department, the notice and hearing process kicks into action. The developer officially has a bullseye put on his back.

While the developer is focused on complying with the filing requirements and preparing for public scrutiny via municipal advisory review boards and/or mandatory community meetings; project opponents covertly prepare and rally their forces under the cover of the notice and hearing process.

The greatest disadvantage that developers have under the notice and hearing system are the rules, which we know, in warfare there are no rules. As we discussed, the opposition needs to instigate conflict to erode the credibility of the applicant, so town hall meetings, public hearings, and workshops provide the perfect platforms for turning these venues into Jerry Springer episodes of conflict. These venues often get hijacked and become spectacles for the news media to report, which kicks off a repeating cycle of negative publicity and social media gnashing of teeth.

The notice and hearing process fails by empowering a sub-set of the community. The homeowners and citizens who attend the meetings often live in close proximity to the proposed project. Therefore, in a community with tens of thousands of citizens, a sub-set of homeowners as few as a dozen can determine the fate of projects that could have benefitted the entire municipality.

Moreover, the opposition is not beholden to the rules of the notice and hearing system. They operate under their own guerilla tactics, demonizing projects with a *political, emotional*, and *chaotic* posture of grassroots engagement that easily trumps the *legal*, *logical*, and *linear* tenets of the system. At the end of the day, a vocal and visible minority of citizens have the upper hand thanks to the notice and hearing system.

THE BRITISH ARE COMING!!

Let me give you an analogy to better link how gossip and the notice hearing process conspires against good real estate development. At the advent the American Revolution, we saw Paul Revere riding across the countryside shouting, "The British are coming, the British are coming."

This is our analogy of gossip with the British army representing a proposed new real estate development navigating the rigid notice and hearing system. The word (gossip) of the advancing British army (proposed project) reaches American colonialists (concerned homeowners) who get ready to resist and fight under their NIMBY "Don't Tread On Me" flag.

The British army, known as the red coats, come marching down the road in orderly columns. They are slow, they are exposed, and they are beholden to tradition or the rules of engagement. The tradition of honorable warfare with rules, where the enemy is met on the battlefield to exchange volleys of fire. This is the notice and hearing construct. It's very linear and constrained, exposing the British army vis-à-vis the developer's application to American militias' guerilla tactics.

The American militia are not wearing bright uniforms, nor are they marching in majestic columns, nor are they carrying flintlock rifles. They are not beholden to the rules of the notice and hearing process. Instead, the opposition takes optimal positions hiding behind trees and stone fences, while occupying the surrounding hills. Where the notice and hearing process arms the British army with flintlock rifles, the rebels are armed with automatic weapons and rocket launchers (today's digital platforms), effectively attacking the red coats from the flanks in a classical military ambush.

This is a very simplified analogy to demonstrate how predictable, lethargic, and antiquated the notice and hearing process is in today's digital universe. The opposition has adapted new technology and tactics, while the overwhelming majority of developers go into communities wearing red coats and marching with bullseyes plastered on their backs.

GUERRILLA WARFARE

If Napoleon was alive today and we asked him to put on his military hat, he would conclude the notice and hearing system created a target-rich environment to carry out ambushes, sabotage, and hijackings! These classic NIMBY maneuvers are part of guerrilla warfare and the NIMBY tool kit. NIMBY opponents are very skilled at bypassing the system to incite *political*, *emotional*, and *chaotic* damage to development projects.

The application rules don't apply to anti-development opponents. In fact, NIMBY forces campaign freely outside of the rules, immune, giving them the advantage over the developer, as well as the process.

As the saying goes, "all's fair in love and war" and the opposition is at war against the developer and the project. For decades, the process unintentionally sets developers up for political gamesmanship that consistently generates public chaos, project crisis, and eventual political defeats for countless projects.

ELEMENT 3: CONVENTIONAL WISDOM

If gossip is the oxygen, and the notice and hearing process the fuel, then conventional wisdom is the spark that sets off NIMBY fires in countless communities across the country. Once a developer has decided to "fly under the radar" it puts into motion the other two elements that ultimately breathes life into the opposition. In short, conventional wisdom abdicates the strategic high ground in the public square. Rumors go unchecked, emotions get heated, and the opposition gets into position to ambush the project as soon as it's filed, if not before.

The bad news is conventional wisdom sparks up the NIMBY fires. The good news is by breaking away from conventional wisdom, developers can begin to acquire greater control over the fate of their projects.

Breaking the conventional wisdom is the key to success in today's digital NIMBY world. The red pill you took in earlier chapters now empowers you to follow the paths of other great innovators and entrepreneurs, and with the help of this book, you can make your own path to greater success. Here are a few leaders who've encouraged us to challenge and break away from conventional wisdom:

Sam Walton, founder of Walmart, "Swim upstream. Go the other way ignore conventional wisdom."

Larry Ellison, founder of Oracle, "The only way to get ahead is find errors in conventional wisdom."

Steven Levitt, economist and author, "The conventional wisdom is often wrong."

Ziad Abdelnour, founder and CEO of Blackhawk Partners, "Challenge conventional wisdom. There is almost always a better way."

In the real estate development industries, there is a better way to engage and neutralize NIMBY forces. You must possess courage and be willing to take risks to break out of the NIMBY Matrix™.

THE RISING THREAT OF NIMBY AVATARS

In the old days, when I was starting out as a public affairs consultant, if someone wanted to oppose a new real estate development, all they needed was a cell phone, an AOL account, and a little determination. These old school NIMBY opponents operated with no budget, no office space, no public relations consultants (usually), no media training, no legal knowledge, and no playbooks.

More often than not, these upstarts organically defeated multi-billion, multi-national corporations with just a few other angry neighbors demonstrating and petitioning their local elected officials.

As we learned, the NIMBY trifecta enabled and empowered tens of thousands of vocal and visible anti-development groups who successfully instigated conflict throughout the application process. Decades before the advent of the internet, Google, and social media, local opposition independently (in most cases) self-organized and mobilized against local projects.

NIMBY opposition would repeat itself in predictable patterns of attacks, which sustained the NIMBY Matrix™ for decades.

THE FIVE TRADITIONAL FACES OF NIMBY

The human condition hasn't changed since before recorded history. I wouldn't doubt that when the Biblical Noah was building his ark, his neighbors were shouting NIMBY to tribe elders.

Status quo attitudes, fueled by the fear of change, runs deep in our DNA and psyche. Over the decades, I've encountered, categorized, and defeated these five different types of NIMBY opponents that projects typically encountered. To better understand the new face of NIMBYism in today's digital age, we must first have a firm grasp of the NIMBY profiles that have laid the foundation throughout the NIMBY Matrix™.

In the January 2005 edition of the Urban Land Institute's publication, *Urban Land Magazine*, I revealed the faces of our everyday NIMBY opponents. In my featured article, Riding the NIMBY Dragan, I shared and broke down the profiles I've been using for years: The Guardian, the Crusader, the Machiavelli, the Watchdog and the Godfather. I believe I even added a bonus profile called the Cranky Crabs. I mention the article to demonstrate that for nearly 20 years, I've been sharing my knowledge and insights for the greater good of our industry.

Surprisingly, these traditional faces of NIMBY haven't changed much, if at all. These NIMBY profiles remain a threat to those who choose the "flying under the radar" posture. However, for those who seek to break out of this false construct, understanding the following profiles gives you a big competitive edge.

THE GUARDIAN (HOMEOWNERS)

The Guardian is responsible for the majority of community conflicts experienced by developers. Guardians are the "neighborhood defenders" of the status quo with deep rooted prejudices they believe defines their community. They are mostly affluent homeowners who make the time to participate in their homeowners' associations, civic groups, and other community activities.

NIMBY Guardians mobilize upon learning about the new development through community grapevine, government notices, or newspaper headlines. The Guardian has always perceived new development as a threat to property values and the character of their communities, as well as traffic congestion and generally anything that threatens to alter the status quo. The Guardian is triggered by scanty information, misperceptions, and faulty communication that stokes the fear of change.

The NIMBY Guardian has been typically a first-time NIMBY opponent who becomes a factor as the public hearing approaches. The sooner the Guardian is engaged by the developer, the better the odds for win-win concessions and dispute resolution.

THE CRUSADER (PROFESSIONAL ACTIVISTS)

The NIMBY Crusader views herself as a champion of a cause rooted in the belief that the environment or the character of the community must prevail over economic progress. Unlike Guardians, who are motivated by the fear of change, Crusaders are motivated by their own moral convictions, and more importantly, the need for self-promotion. Most Crusaders are environmentalists, conservationists, and preservationists who believe the cost of change and new development is too high a price to pay.

NIMBY Crusaders are professionals representing special interest groups who cater to dues-paying members who want to see action, which is spurred on by news headlines, grassroots activism, and public conflict. The Crusader carries the flag of NIMBY in part to protect the status quo, but also to promote the organization or the individual activist in order to enhance their political clout, fundraising, and membership drives.

NIMBY Crusaders see corporate real estate development as providing not only an opportunity to claim the moral high ground, but also to raise their own profiles for financial gain. They have little-to-no incentive to mediate a compromise when they see blood in the water.

THE MACHIAVELLI (POLITICAL OPPORTUNISTS)

The NIMBY Machiavelli are politically motivated and adept at exploiting community anxieties to promote their own self-serving agenda. They promote their media profile so they can vie for a seat in the next local election or some other high-profile position.

The NIMBY Machiavelli reside in every community and sometimes are former Guardians who enjoyed basking in the media spotlight and seeing their name in the newspaper. In other cases, NIMBY Machiavelli is a Crusader who is a first-time candidate or a self-appointed "throw the bums out" citizen activist who has run for office in the past.

The Machiavelli usually leaves his or her fingerprints on the community and should be identified as part of the developer's effort to prevent inflammatory voices in the wilderness from reaching the media. It is worth noting that elected officials appreciate a developer who preempts and manages the Machiavellian agenda, giving them political cover from these political antagonists.

Note: Sometimes the NIMBY Machiavelli are elected officials themselves who are vying for higher office. For example, if a city commissioner wants to be the next mayor and the current mayor supports your project, more often than not in that scenario, the Machiavelli commissioner will oppose the project and call upon opposition to weaken the mayor, while co-opting the populist anti-development position.

THE WATCHDOG (LOCAL REPORTERS)

The NIMBY Watchdog is the local government beat reporter assigned to cover public hearings. Conflict sells newspaper and television advertising, which is why the news media is primed to showcase the next David versus Goliath battle. The news media typically favors NIMBY causes because the homeowner is not only perceived as the underdog, but also because they, the NIMBY opposition, contacts the press first, creating an immediate narrative and bias against the developer.

THE GODFATHER (HYBRID)

There are hybrids and extensions borne out of the first four traditional faces of NIMBY. One being the NIMBY Godfather. This person has established himself as a successful opponent, defeating a project or a series of projects. He has gained some news and social media celebrity, as well as political influence that has attracted other likeminded anti-development groups.

For example, it's not uncommon to see multiple homeowner associations form an alliance to deter and attack future projects. We see homeowner association presidents assign their power to one person to be essentially the Godfather representing their collective self interests. Developers and elected officials are expected to kiss the ring of these Godfathers, which puts these communities under a status quo lockdown.

THE DAWN OF DIGITAL NIMBY

Today, more than ever, it's easy to spread gossip, incite protests, cancel adversaries, and instigate conflicts thanks to digital media. The internet has brought ease and accessibility to global information. However, it doesn't mean that we're informed when it comes to possessing "the truth".

Today, we live and operate in echo chambers that reinforce and validate our current values, beliefs, and attitudes. An echo chamber is where we gather our information, exercise commerce, and find our entertainment. It's also where we actively shut out platforms and voices that don't pass our filters for truth, preferences, and sincerity.

For example: If you're politically liberal, then your likely news sources are The New York Times, Washington Post and CNN. If you're politically conservative, then Fox News Channel, talk radio, and the Wall Street Journal underwrites your echo chamber construct.

For the purposes of *Breaking Out of the NIMBY Matrix™*, I'm going to focus on Facebook, where the vast majority of NIMBY opposition resides and operates. Facebook has been the center of most, if not all, of the echo chambers in our society today. In the last 10 years, we've seen Facebook become one of the top destinations on the internet. Google, Facebook, and YouTube are the top three visited sites throughout the globe.

NIMBY opponents have not only adopted the tools of the Digital Age, but have become digital NIMBY activists via social media platforms such as Facebook. They've successfully created echo chambers of opposition in every real estate development industry. Their influence is an X-factor that sustains and expands the NIMBY Matrix™.

THE RISE OF NIMBY AVATARS

I have seen on Facebook hundreds of NIMBY-based groups actively opposing real estate development projects across the nation. These groups range from a few dozen to thousands of anti-development followers. I wouldn't doubt the numbers of Facebook groups would number in the thousands, but again, no one is formally studying this area of burgeoning opposition.

Facebook creates these echo chambers elevating the digital NIMBY activism at the grassroots level. They have also emboldened and digitally amplified the traditional profiles of Guardians, Crusaders, and Machiavelli, which I now profile them as NIMBY Avatars.

NIMBY Avatars are a new breed of anti-development opposition. They are still one of the traditional faces of NIMBY (Guardian, Crusader etc.), but now they have a digital stage and spotlight. They have a captivated and motivated audience that shares the same angst, fears, and perceptions towards new development. Additionally, they can literally share the negative content on their social media feeds, reaching more people.

Moreover, they have Facebook pages focused on opposing a specific project or company. They now have unchecked power enabling them to blatantly mischaracterize facts, spread false claims, and peddle their so-called "Google-Based Science," which is mostly slanted opinions and unvetted blog reports.

NIMBY Avatars operate without any accountability in the digital public square. If someone opposes their opinions on a Facebook post, they're either vilified by other followers or simply blocked from the Facebook page. I've seen firsthand pro-project residents or citizens advocating for my client's projects by countering opposition's false facts, citing proven data, to be virtually attacked and vilified: public discourse doesn't serve the NIMBY Avatars' objectives.

NIMBY Avatars believe their own self-generated press and see themselves as populists, even though their Facebook page followers are either a small number or mostly comprised of followers from outside their communities.

When these NIMBY Avatars actually show up to public hearings and meetings, they strut around as if they walk on water, expecting to be greeted much like royalty. They're full of hubris and arrogance. It's a sad reality that repeatedly manifests itself in the NIMBY Matrix™, and it's only getting worse.

THE NIMBY MATRIX™ IS HIDING A TROUBLING TREND

NIMBY Avatars and their Facebook opposition groups have grown in power, influence, and reach. You better believe that local officials visit their pages, comb through the comments, and see who is liking every post. For every pro-project comment, if any dare, there are 10 anti-development responses attacking the person who went up against the group. These Facebook groups have become almost militant, and any expressed doubts by group members are met with quick and derisive aggression. Digitally speaking, they're never heard from again.

NIMBY Avatars are unquestioned and they're the unchallenged lords of the land. Their narratives are very hard to ignore if you're an elected official or member of the news media. Their censored echo chambers mostly convey a false reality that manifests into political trouble for corporate developers and their applications.

A GROWING CONCERN

What's emerging as a troubling trend, that's only whispered in certain parts of the NIMBY Matrix™, is the networking and expansion of these Facebook opposition groups. We're seeing more and more Facebook groups swimming like rogue sharks seeking out other projects to attack once they're finished with the initial project. It's not restricted to the local community either.

I've encountered NIMBY Avatars forging alliances with their counterparts across state lines and across the nation. They conduct recon on companies in their neck of the woods and report to the other opposition groups that's opposing in another market.

In increasing fashion, we're seeing 501(C)(4)s feeding local Facebook opposition groups with playbooks filled with strategies, tactics, messaging, and grassroots tools and templates. Who are behind these C4s depends on the industry, but you can make an educated guess who it is, and won't be too far off. I'll give you a hint – follow the money that secretly goes into these groups.

The greatest ally to these NIMBY Avatars is no one is paying attention to their growing influence, power, and reach. The NIMBY Matrix™ has successfully distracted developers who don't see or want to see the bigger picture. However, I've come across a growing number of corporate professionals who have witnessed and experienced this troubling trend. It's real and it is in the early stages of maturation.

The more this information gets out and discussed, the less influence these NIMBY Avatars will have in the public square. That's my hope at least and why I wrote this book. More professionals who adopt a red pill perspective, the more likely we can change the current false realities hurting good people and projects.

PRODUCE YOUR OWN FACEBOOK PROJECT PAGE

The good news is you can effectively counter by putting up your own pro-project Facebook group pages. The public has a right to learn the merits of the project and the company that's applying for the license to operate. You'd be surprised of the impact of putting up a Facebook page. If done correctly, you can have *more* people follow your page than the opposition. Not every time, but more often than you would think. I've had more than a few Facebook group pages win the numbers of likes and follows optics, which elected officials' noticed.

How do you know if your Facebook page is getting the job done?

You know that your Facebook page is reaching and influencing stakeholders when the opposition feels compelled to attack your page. Typically, they will post on their Facebook pages your Facebook content. In their minds, they're attacking you, but in reality, they're repeating your messaging before their audience, which is a small victory. It's a small victory, because by posting your content, they're breaking down their echo chamber and letting in your narrative, which is always a win.

There's best practices that you can exercise, but suffice it to say, you determine what is discussed on your Facebook page and what impressions you want to convey. The opposition has their Facebook forum to misinform, confuse, and stoke anger, so that doesn't mean you have to allow them, to invade your Facebook page to disrupt your attempts to post positive, accurate information.

Your Facebook page can have a disclaimer that anyone who comments for the purposes of being purely argumentative, accusatory, and disrespectful to other followers and their comments, will be banned from the page. Public discourse is a commodity and thoughtfully posted comments offering questions or even rational arguments questioning the project should be welcomed and appreciated.

Certainly, the elected officials notice the constructive exchanges in this public square that you have created.

Keep this in mind, when NIMBY Avatars are attacking your Facebook page with disrespectful comments, while also attempting to discredit your Facebook page on their anti-project Facebook page, you're effectively taking them off message and putting them on the defensive. Not to mention, exposing their self-serving arrogance in full digital display.

THE DARK SIDE OF NIMBY MATRIX

Unfortunately, there's a dark side to NIMBY opposition within the NIMBY Matrix™. This dark side can be found in the inner reaches of the human condition, which lacks character, courage, and compassion. This dark side is sustained by ignorance and fear, and yet, it goes mostly ignored and unspoken in the throes of battle at city hall.

Over my career, I've seen it in action in full display and disgust. The threats of changing the community heightens its effects and spreads it like a disease. If you haven't figured it out by now, I'm talking about racism followed closely by elitism and fearism.

Racism, elitism, and fearism drives the dark side of NIMBYism in the NIMBY Matrix™. It's never pretty when it manifests itself, but as I've mentioned, it largely goes ignored, but it's the elephant in the room in too many cases of NIMBY controversies.

I'm not a psychologist or a sociologist, but it doesn't take a rocket scientist to know you cannot always take NIMBY opposition at face value. When you look beyond the façade and decipher the coded messaging, you will see an uglier side of our neighbors who rally to protect the "character of their communities".

RACISM

Let me be clear and emphasize not all NIMBY opponents are racist, but on the same token, not all NIMBY opponents are pure as the driven snow. When it comes to affordable, low-cost housing or apartments, affluent homeowners aren't going to openly admit their prejudices. However, the signs of racism are there if you're looking for it.

Occasionally, we'll see homeowners let their guards down in opposing projects by saying "Build it where THEY live!". In other scenarios, they'll slip and say, "We don't want a Walmart, but we'll support a new Target."

In those cases involving racist motivations, racism is laced within coded language that disguises the dark side. For example, affordable housing triggers deep rooted fears and anger. Instead of saying they don't want a certain demographic to live in their neighborhood, which would be racist, NIMBY opponents will speak in code arguing these projects will "increase the crime rate", "decrease property values", "overcrowd our schools" and "increase traffic".

These coded messages are conveyed with passion and anger that leads to a mob-like fury. The local news media reports it word-for-word, and public officials accept it at face value. In nearly every instance these coded messages are delivered by affluent homeowners.

Unsurprisingly, there aren't enough academic, or industry studies conducted on this terrible display of the human condition. So, it's par of the course in the NIMBY Matrix™.

ELITISM

When affluent homeowners aren't motivated by racism, they'll exhibit elitist qualities in the name of NIMBY. I'll give three examples of elitism or classism.

Workforce housing is another problem in America. Most firefighters, police officers, and nurses cannot afford to live in the urban communities where they work. They often must find affordable housing in other cities or even neighboring counties. They, like most of us, want to raise their families in safe communities with good schools, without having to commute hours every day. I've seen more than my fair share of good quality multi-family housing projects or apartment complexes get defeated by neighboring homeowners, claiming their coded arguments.

Another example is bankrupted gated golf-course communities. Thousands of these golf courses have closed down, leaving homeowners with expansive backyards of green space and private enjoyment. When a developer comes in proposing new housing or condominiums, which is known as infill, the homeowners living on the dilapidated golf course revolt to keep their private green spaces to themselves.

In a beach community on the east side of Florida, a hotel developer client experienced neighborhood opposition to his proposed hotel. The hotel was a nationally respected, high quality brand name, and the location was already zoned as a community redevelopment area (CRA), so this hotel project met the current zoning laws.

However, the homeowners, who lived within the CRA, who knew they lived in the CRA, opposed the hotel. Their excuse was a large oak tree that was in the middle of blighted lot filled with trash, shopping carts, car batteries, and the occasionally bum. The local merchants supported the hotel project because tourists were having to go to other beach communities to find hotel rooms, which reduced their foot traffic. We prevailed after a few months of engaging the community.

FEARISM

Most of us have an aversion to losing what we have in our possession, which includes the character of our community or the devil we know. When a new development threatens to change the look or feel of our community, then a fear of change kicks in turning good neighbors into threatened defenders of the status quo. This is a natural response that leads to negative emotions and anxieties.

Neighbors, who hear from the community grapevine the mischaracterizations, or half truths about a project, scrap circumspection and act on impulsive anger. Neighbors aren't entirely at fault for defaulting to this posture, which we touched upon in prior chapters.

Yet, the fear of change is a powerful motivator and instigator undermining any semblance of public discourse. Angry homeowners who feel betrayed or ignored become a force that sustains the NIMBY Matrix™.

WE'RE ALL NIMBYS!

Every one of us has some elements of NIMBY within us. The uncertainty or fear that comes with change is intrinsic and part of what makes us, well us. It doesn't help when the NIMBY Matrix™ presents change in a less than empowering context. I can honestly say if I had learned about a proposed methadone clinic or landfill being considered down the road from my neighborhood, I would greet this information with a less than an understandable attitude.

In fact, I'd be ticked off that I had to hear about it through the grapevine versus being invited by the municipality or developer to participate in the planning process. I've been a part of many constructive dialogues with ardent opponents, which have led to smart concessions by the developer, creating equitable mediation in many cases.

For the record, I have helped a few clients oppose projects, which I've been very successful.

One project was a proposed toll road going through a nearby rural county in Florida. If built, the toll road would have changed the rural character of the community and kill off downtown businesses with the bypass. Most troubling, when the toll road route was mapped out, no one at the state level ever spoke with county leaders or local public officials. The fate of an entire county was being decided upon by outside special interests who had no cares for this particular county.

My point here not every NIMBY opponent is unreasonable or nefarious. As I said, not every affluent homeowner or NIMBY opponent are operating with certain biases or prejudices, but rather, operating out of anger from being ignored and dismissed by the process.

DEVELOPERS CAN BE ELITISTS TOO

The dark side of NIMBYism cuts both ways. Corporate developers can get trapped in their own success. Moreover, developers fear community pushback on their projects, so they decide to "fly under the radar" to avoid detection, which leaves third parties or neighbors in the dark.

To be more direct, developers are guilty of their own elitism.

They approach the municipality or community with a degree of arrogance or indifference to community concerns. They'll only initiate a community dialogue if the municipality mandates public outreach. This favors the NIMBY Matrix™ and as we've learned so far, only creates community anxieties and anger that brings out, at best angry homeowners, and at worse hateful homeowners screaming NIMBY.

THE RABBIT HOLE

My goal for Breaking Out of the NIMBY Matrix™ is to help minimize the incidents of community anger, marginalize agents of hate, and maximize the potential for true citizen engagement. It cannot be done without landing at the bottom of the rabbit hole, taking it in, and now preparing to climb out of it.

Let's spend the rest of this book, exploring how you can control your reality and outcomes in the NIMBY Matrix™.

PART II

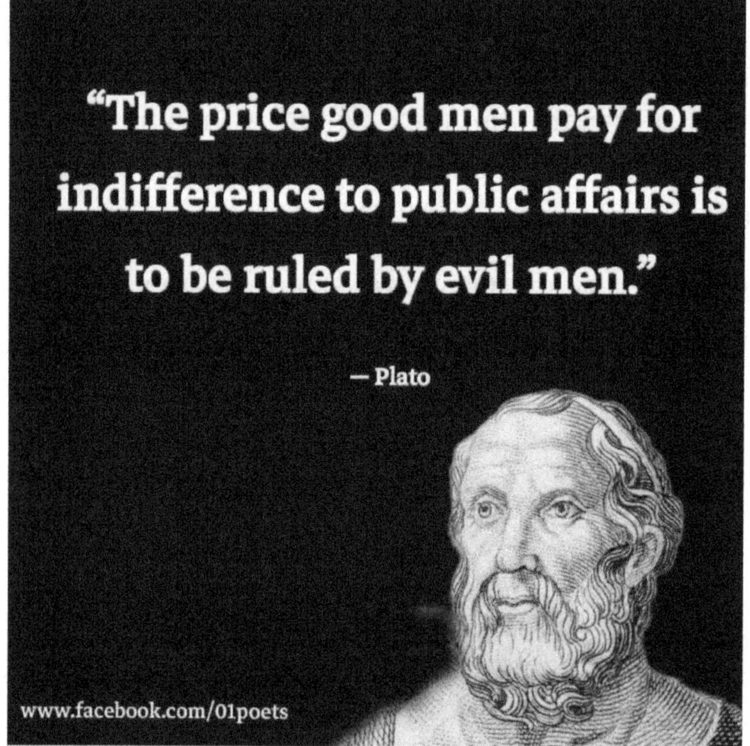

"The price good men pay for indifference to public affairs is to be ruled by evil men."
— Plato
www.facebook.com/01poets

OPPORTUNITY KNOCKS

"Innovation is the ability to see change as an opportunity – not a threat."

Steve Jobs

Congratulations for making it to this point in the book! It's not easy to break out of the NIMBY Matrix™, but you've escaped it. The question now is how do you capitalize on new opportunities with your newly found perspective?

I'll be the first to tell you that it's not easy, and it's not for those with weak constitutions. However, for those who dare to break away from conventional thinking, opportunities will knock at your door. After reading the remainder of the book, you'll have a competitive edge over not only your colleagues, but anti-development forces who have banked on conventional wisdom.

I want to share a client success story that didn't happen overnight. It was years in the making. One of my clients operates in the renewable energy development industry. Over the last several years, renewable energy (solar and wind), has become one of the most contested industries in the development space: NIMBY opposition is intensive, digitally networked, and defeating a lot of local projects.

My client wanted to break away from the "fly under the radar" construct, realizing that it had become more a hindrance than a solution. Over the course of several years, we incrementally built on successes, lessons learned, and putting new tools in the public affairs toolbox – one project at a time. Ultimately, the client decided to be "less timid" and more aggressive in grassroots citizen engagement campaigns.

After years of small, but significant successes of changing internal cultures, status quo attitudes, and project victories, we reached the corporate mindset of engaging the community regardless of NIMBY opposition. This was a big step for my client. Hell, a big step for any company that is accustomed to keeping a low profile.

KNOCK, KNOCK – WHO'S THERE?

Let me share a success story. We had a solar permit that was months away from being filed with the local municipality in a Midwest rural township. I recommended to the client that we knock on doors to introduce our company and our project to the neighbors who will be 500 feet or less from the proposed solar facility. I credit the client for taking the risk and trusting my counsel to go for it. Up to this point, there was no indication of opposition. Again, this trust was built up over several years of working on multiple projects, so it wasn't an arbitrary recommendation or decision.

The results were amazing!

In two days, the land agent and I knocked on over 100 doors. Over 50 percent of the doors we knocked on, we spoke with the homeowners. Over half already heard through the grapevine about the project, but they haven't spoken seriously with anyone, so fears hadn't reached anxiety level. We handed homeowners a one-page summary of our company with pre-emptive messaging that mitigated the predictable unfounded allegations of devaluing property values, environmental harm, and optics. Only one door was shut in our face out of the 100 door knocks, which is an incredible outcome.

However, the most surprising outcome was when the land agent and I knocked at the door of a couple whose home would be completely surrounded by solar fields. As we began approaching the front porch, we commented to one another how we heard the couple being very angry and hostile to the proposal. In all honesty, I wasn't looking forward to knocking on this door.

As we came up on the porch, we were greeted by the lady of the house. Once we introduced ourselves, she didn't hold back her anger or her tears of frustration. Admittedly, it wasn't ideal to be standing on the front porch with the lady of the home crying in public view, but it quickly got better.

Despite her wanting to kick us off the porch, she accepted our offer to sit down in the backyard for just a few minutes.

We discussed who we were, and what this project was about, and to see how we as "good neighbors" can find a win-win scenario.

What started out as a diatribe turned into a polite conversation that led to several more meetings over the next few weeks with her and her spouse. We discovered in our conversations the couple believed via the grapevine that the solar fencing was going to be right on their property line (40 feet from their back porch). In fact, the fencing and project would be nearly a football field away. This was a turning point. The client offered to increase the buffering that included the lady's request for fruit trees. The client agreed to this and several other workable concessions.

In the end, the neighbor who had the most to lose, in their minds, turned out to be the most supportive of the project. Also, we didn't know until we broke bread on that front porch that the homeowners' and neighboring farmer had a long troubled feud, so our association with the farmer, who leased his land to us, made us guilty by association in their eyes vis-à-vis we had no credibility.

Our door knocking not only developed crucial credibility, but it pre-empted subsequent efforts of neighbors who eventually tried to rally opposition. They were unsuccessful due to our transparency, and our good neighbor citizen engagement initiative that resulted in securing "goodwill" social capital.

In fact, the one neighbor who unsuccessfully tried to rally opposition, gave up, so he put his house up for sale. He moved out in less than two months. Ironically, his location would have barely seen any solar panels in the far off distance.

THE BIGGER PICTURE

The moral of this success story is you must be willing to fight off the fear of failure by always playing it safe. Certainly, the door knocking could have gone the opposite direction, but it didn't. Matter of fact, several homeowners asked to be included in the project, leasing their land. Moreover, we got ahead of the grapevine and would-be opponents to the project. The solar project was unanimously approved and not one NIMBY opponent attended the public hearings.

The brass tacks are this: It's better to create NIMBYism under your terms than wait for the hammer to drop on your project. The differentiator is you're showcasing good neighbor transparency that establishes enduring credibility. Over 80 percent of NIMBYism that comes out of the NIMBY Trifecta is based on misinformation and mischaracterizations.

Neighbors need credible and accessible information, which in most cases isn't provided by developers and applicants. This is a significant area of opportunity for corporate developers. The public square is there for the taking for those developers and land-use professionals willing to seize the opportunity to occupy it.

OPPORTUNITY IN BITE SIZES

Red pill successes in a digital NIMBY world happens incrementally. You now have the public affairs toolbox, but you need to start developing the tools necessary to be consistently successful. This will take time, which is ideal.

The great news is you'll be able to see the chessboard with much more clarity and certainty.

THE POLITICS OF REAL ESTATE DEVELOPMENT

We must start this chapter agreeing that real estate development is a political enterprise. You can peel away the impressive financing, legal rights, and the smart- growth planning, but at its core, real estate development is a political blood sport. It's political because you must secure the majority, in some cases, supermajority, vote from municipal public officials at the township, city, and county levels.

Former Speaker of the House of Representatives Tip O'Neill coined the phrase, "All politics is local", which has proven true for generations. Nothing triggers political controversy at the local level more than real estate projects that threaten the status quo, fear of change, and ignorant prejudices. In turn, nothing causes elected officials more apprehension and stress than angry homeowners threatening to vote them out of office should they vote in favor of a controversial development.

It doesn't matter what type of application is being sought or by what real estate development industry. The politics of real estate development equally threatens site plans, entitlements, rezoning, and permitting. Emotions trump logic. Politics undermines legal. Chaos clouds certainty. Local elected officials who want to remain in office can get very political, very quickly, if they believe their seats are threatened.

Therefore, elected officials experiencing NIMBY duress become hard pressed when determining the fate of proposed master-planned communities, sub-divisions, mixed use, mining operations, solar and wind farms, new malls, skyscrapers, big boxes, multi-family apartments, infill (e.g. abandoned golf courses), hospitals, prisons, landfills, airports, hotels, and affordable housing every day. More often than not, public policy is decided within this political shooting gallery.

If you can agree with me, then we can astutely discuss what is public affairs and why it's essential in winning more project approvals at the local level.

WHAT IS PUBLIC AFFAIRS?

Public affairs is the fraternal twin to public relations. Both engage the news media. Both develop persuasive messaging that frames stakeholder impressions. Both generate positive publicity, while rapidly mitigating negative stories vis-à-vis crisis communications. Both integrate the best of many disciplines such as marketing communications, branding, social and digital media, websites, media relations, internal communications, investor relations, paid media, and video communications.

The one big difference is public relations is more business-to-business (B2B) and business-to-consumer (B2C) focused, while public affairs is solely focused on influencing public policy at the municipal, state, and federal government levels. Public affairs is essential to what we call "the process" of making the sausage.

I've worked as a public affairs professional for more than 25 years. I've directly influenced public policy in more than 20 states, as well as federal policy including the War on Terror. The better public affairs operatives are adept at performing multiple aspects of persuasion and influence including building alliances, managing coalitions, conducting grassroots advocacy, holding pressers at the state capitol, briefing capital press reporters, ghostwriting and placing guest columns, conducting editorial (ed) board meetings, coordinating speakers' bureaus, and working hand-to-glove with government relations professionals a.k.a. lobbyists.

The practice of passing or killing legislation with public affairs is not much different at the municipal level when it comes to the approval process. I admit that my prior experience as a Florida mayor, has given me a unique perspective in conducting public affairs at the local level. If I didn't possess that perspective, experience, and first-hand knowledge, then I wouldn't have been any different than the other public affairs operatives down the street.

PUBLIC AFFAIRS AND NIMBY

The lack of public affairs strategies, tactics, and integrated best practices explains why the NIMBY Matrix™ gets a pass. For decades, NIMBY opponents have enjoyed the strategic high ground, while dictating their cadence of conflict until the final vote is counted.

Unfortunately, most self-professed public relations operatives who assert they can help developers defeat NIMBYism present little to no experience in the public affairs field. That doesn't mean there aren't a few who know what they're doing such as political consultants and former legislators or commissioners, but even they lack the integrated experience needed to defeat NIMBYism in today's digital world.

Admittedly, as a corporate consultant and public affairs quarterback, I've enjoyed a competitive advantage and a unique selling position. However, I've grown frustrated with seeing how easily NIMBY activists manipulate other good projects and good, reputable companies who try to do the right thing in the public square.

That is why I've written Part II. In order to help others successfully break out of the NIMBY Matrix™, we need better practices, better campaigns, and better professionals taking on savvy NIMBY opponents who operate largely unchallenged in the NIMBY Matrix™.

PUBLIC AFFAIRS OR BUST

It may have seemed I was knocking the few professionals out there who are trying to cobble together public affairs efforts to help defeat NIMBYism for their clients. On the contrary, we need more public affairs professionals who can *effectively* contribute to a developer's A-team of land-use lawyers, planners, brokers, agents, and marketing/PR specialists. Also, educating developers and land-use professionals on recognizing and managing the benefits of integrated public affairs.

I've had the pleasure of working with many political consultants and a few former state legislators on real estate development projects. They have a better than average understanding on how to lobby local leaders and influence the news media, but often the client requires added skillsets to effectively integrate public affairs for optimal influence.

In the forthcoming pages, I've laid out my equation for success and model for integrating public affairs that deceases the risks of public rejection, while increasing the odds for project approvals.

May the forthcoming pages inspire a new generation of professionals who are ready to make a positive change in the real estate development industry.

THE A=CE^2 EQUATION FOR GREATER SUCCESS

For you to be more successful in defeating NIMBYism, it's not enough to know that you're operating under the thumb of the NIMBY Matrix™. You need a profound, yet simple equation to break away and dismantle the NIMBY Matrix™ once and for all.

It begins with *Integrated Public Affairs* (IPA), which takes the best of multiple communications and grassroots disciplines. There are many ways to reach and influence a coalition of audiences spanning crisis management, legal counsel, grassroots advocacy, corporate communications, public relations, social and digital media, political marketing, video communications, speakers' bureau, community briefings, and media relations.

Integrated Public Affairs is a new field of stakeholder influence, practiced by a very small circle of capable professionals. The bad news is that circle of expertise gets significantly smaller when you're in the NIMBY Matrix™. The good news is I'm going to share my simple equation that will underwrite your future IPA campaigns, giving you the right balance of IPA that's not too much or too little, but just right.

EQUATION FOR MORE SUCCESS

The secret to creating and executing a successful integrated public affairs operation is applying my equation $A=CE^2$ (Approvals = Citizen Engagement²). Projects have a greater chance of getting *approvals* when integrated public affairs takes the best of *traditional citizen engagement* and combines it with *digital citizen engagement*. Thus, you get the simple equation of $A=CE^2$ (Approvals = Citizen Engagement²) in your integrated public affairs initiatives.

Think of integrated public affairs as an eighteen wheeler and my $A=CE^2$ equation as the big motor powering the rig down the highway. As we will see, an effective integrated public affairs operation or campaign based on my $A=CE^2$ equation will secure the social and political capital you need to win.

Let's take a closer look at the respective communications and citizen engagement disciplines to have a better understanding of how to activate my $A=CE^2$ equation. Each one of these disciplines operate and influence stakeholders encapsulated in the equation driving IPA.

CRISIS MANAGEMENT

The first rule in crisis management is not making a bad situation worse. The crisis usually begins when the NIMBY hits the fan creating negative publicity, social media attacks, allies scrambling for cover, public officials under political duress, and the opposition smelling blood in the water. The pressure to "do something" to help allies and public officials is intense.

The answer is not hosting a town hall meeting, which developers almost always default to. This only gives the opposition another opportunity to create a media spectacle to intensify conflict that further weakens your credibility and the project's viability.

Crisis management is about minimizing the target on your back, falling back, and regrouping. The opposition is expecting you to come out into the open for the kill shot, so don't give them what they're expecting, instead, be unorthodox and unpredictable.

LEGAL COUNSEL

We will go more in-depth on *Leveling Up Your Legal Game* in the next chapter with my good friend Brian Seymour, Esq., but it must be said no integrated public affairs campaign can be successful without a legal strategy and critical path. This is generally prepared by the land-use lawyer who understands the legal and political elements that affect the pending application. The lawyer has the relationships in the planning department and the elected officials themselves.

However, land-use lawyers are not equipped to develop and execute an integrated public affairs campaign. They are the generals who command the battles, but they're rarely seen on the field of battle, which is a good thing. Many good lawyers will tell you if they're the face of the project, then the NIMBY Matrix™ has the upper hand.

CORPORATE COMMUNICATIONS

Corporate communications is often found within publicly held or multi-national companies who communicate with their shareholders, investors, industry and mainstream news media, customers, vendors, partners, and employees. Corporate communications is entrusted with safeguarding the reputation and image of the company and its C-suite executives. We typically see corporate communications department far removed from the gamesmanship and blood sport of local real estate politics.

However, when the credibility of the company is under attack, corporate communications can play a supportive role in communicating that the community-at-large is an important corporate stakeholder, granting the local license to operate. Corporate communications can be an effective channel of communicating the company's commitment to citizen engagement in the public square. In other words, they're an underutilized and overlooked resource of influence.

PUBLIC RELATIONS

There's a difference between promoting a product or service to customers and influencing the legislators who make public policy. The latter is public affairs, while the former is public relations. That said, there are some crossover skillsets from public relations that empowers any public affairs endeavor.

In public relations, we always start with the audience first. We build our campaigns around the messaging that reaches and resonates with our targeted audiences. This is where public relations and public affairs combines for optimal effect. In this case, the targeted audience are the public officials who will be voting on the application. There are other stakeholders who must be influenced as well to include community and business leaders, civic opinion leaders, bloggers, editors, reporters, and the community-at-large.

Message development is a crucial element to any successful citizen engagement initiative. At a minimum, a message box must be developed. It begins with four basic sections answering the following questions:

1. What Do We Say About Ourselves?
2. What Do We Say About the Project?
3. What Does the Opposition Say About Themselves?
4. What Does the Opposition Say When Attacking Us?

Looking at the more advanced levels of public relations, which underwrites integrated public affairs is positioning the *company to define the project* instead of the *project defining the company.* The latter is often accomplished by the opposition to discrediting and demonizing the project first. This is why we want to be as proactive and early as possible. Again, the NIMBY trifecta rarely witnesses these advance stages of public relations and public affairs, giving an edge to anyone who dares to go against the NIMBY Matrix™.

Lastly, public relations prepares media kits for handouts and online pdfs comprised of statements, reports, releases, bios, guest columns, as well as frequently asked questions, fact sheets, endorsements, brochures, one-pagers, and other informative documents that effectively educate reporters and other stakeholders.

MEDIA RELATIONS

Nothing threatens a project's chances for approval more than negative publicity. A typical negative news story has a headline that includes "Neighbors Mobilize to Oppose Developer or _____ Development" with the leader of the opposition quoted in the top third of the story, while the developer is quoted at the bottom third. In the middle, the mayor or public official is put on the spot, being asked, on how they're going to vote? They either speak against the project or they call for town hall meetings, delays, or expensive concessions that make the project financially unviable.

Such news stories are boilerplate, empowering the opposition, antagonizing public officials, and putting developers on the defensive. Yet, it's not entirely the reporter's fault for the negative publicity. Seriously, how can it be the reporter's fault when they hear first from the opposition with their effective pitching and uncontested framing, while hearing crickets from the applicant?

Reporters are often manipulated by the opposition, which is standard operating procedure. In my experience, if you get to the reporter before the opposition or have press documents already in the queue ready to go, you have a better than fair chance of getting a fair to favorable news story. Not every time, but certainly more often compared to waiting for the reporter's call late in the afternoon when the negative story has mostly been written and they just need a token quote from the developer.

GRASSROOTS ADVOCACY

When it comes to grassroots or third-party advocacy, I have a time tested saying, "It's not what you say as the applicant, but who says it for you." Every project has natural allies in the community. They can be recruited in local chambers, merchants' groups, Rotaries and Kiwanis Clubs, homebuilders, labor unions, realtor boards, and various charitable boards and organizations. Sometimes they're homeowner association board members, former elected officials, or the owners of the property being developed.

Surprisingly, most developers ignore this opportunity to engage leaders in the community and recruit them to publicly support the project with letters to elected officials and editors, submitting guest columns to the local newspaper, and speaking in support at public hearings. By asking for their support, you get a great ally and voice supporting the project.

Moreover, when being interviewed by a reporter, the developer is now empowered to direct the reporter to one or several leaders in the community who will be interviewed endorsing the project. This is a proven tactic that takes away column inches from the opposition's negative comments and providing supportive endorsements that reassure local officials.

One last note, even if you fail to win over community leaders to publicly support your project, you may have successfully neutralized them from speaking out against your project in the public square.

This is very effective approach. Years ago, I helped get a landfill approved, not by recruiting advocates, but educating community leaders who remained neutral, which was a win.

Meeting with community leaders checks the boxes of citizen engagement and affirms your company's commitment to being a good corporate neighbor and citizen.

It gives you positive optics regardless of whom you engage in the public square to include the opposition. We'll get more in detail on this in the Fist in Velvet Glove chapter.

DIGITAL AND SOCIAL MEDIA ACTIVISM

Social media has significantly contributed to the rise of digital activism that's comprised of websites, blogs, fundraisers, petition drives, apps, and videos. Traditional citizen engagement strategies must include digital citizen engagement elements in order to counter and compete for the attention of key audiences.

No doubt, Facebook has leveled up the opposition's reach and influence at the local level. It has become standard operating procedure for opponents to put up an anti-project Facebook page. Even more concerning, we're seeing and increasing trend of local Facebook anti-development groups aligning with other Facebook anti-development groups, forming regional and even national networks of anti-development activists. Such alliances share their best practices, tactics, messaging, and "how-to" playbooks.

Even when the local project is defeated, these Facebook anti-development groups continue to operate, seeking out other projects to NIMBY. Developers who approach the public square with no digital citizen engagement plans are simply abdicating the strategic digital high ground to NIMBY avatars, not to mention inviting inevitable controversy.

Case in point: When rumors go around about the project or future use of the property...what do most people do when they're concerned and curious? That's right, they Google search. In the world of the NIMBY Matrix™, concerned citizens will typically find the opposition's basic website, Facebook page, negative news stories, or blog postings.

Rarely do they come across any developer-sponsored or pro-project links on the web. It doesn't take an Einstein to surmise what people take away from their online searches about the project.

Digital citizen engagement is a key component to the $A=CE^2$ equation. It levels up and compounds the effectiveness of traditional or grassroots citizen engagement. The community-at-large is entitled to know more about your company, your body of work, your reasons for proposing the pending project, the merits of the pending project, what are the benefits, and who supports it.

We'll learn more about digital media and citizen engagement with digital media genius Jennings DePriest in an upcoming chapter dedicated to this topic. For now, suffice it to say, an integrated public affairs campaign is anchored by a minimum of a project-centric website or landing page, a basic press kit for downloading, and how to contact your elected officials' advocacy page.

A side note on the benefits of using a project website. On one project, the opposition attempted to blindside the client by calling in a TV news crew. The reporter didn't call my client at first, but instead checked out our project website and located one of the farmers we featured in the video on our homepage. The reporter tracked down the farmer in our video, and the farmer did a great job refuting the reporter's attacks and even questioning the opponent's motivations. Even better, the reporter used some of the positive video shots from our website for the story.

In this case, we decided not to pursue the reporter to insert a client statement. We didn't need to.

What could have been a typical negative TV news story of local opponents fighting an out of town developer, turned into locals voicing differences over our proposed project. It was hardly a positive news story, but because of our project website and our farmer partner, we changed the narrative and brought the coverage to a more balanced story that had minimal impact on our targeted stakeholders.

POLITICAL MARKETING

Integrated public affairs has a political marketing element that underwrites your citizen engagement best practices. At the end of the day, you're trying to earn and secure a majority vote by a local body of elected, or in some cases, appointed officials. This explains why we see developers retain political consultants to be part of the A-team. However, they have their limitations.

Political consultants have great influence and access to the elected officials. That doesn't necessarily mean they will lobby hard to get your project approved. The elected officials are their gravy trains offering continuous sources of income as they run for re-election or higher office. Your project is essentially a one off for political consultants, so they're not going to burn bridges.

I've seen a very influential political consultant turn down $50,000 to directly lobby their client, the mayor, who was the swing vote, to vote in favor of a controversial project. They walked away from the check and the project.

Also, it's worth noting that political campaigns are geared to polarize and wedge voters, and not building consensus. Therefore, political marketing has limited benefits, but there are a few tactics that empower citizen engagement and educating the public square.

Political marketing offers direct mail, texting, door knocking, opinion polling, focus groups, yard signs, ads (print, TV/radio, social media), and political action committees; all essential tools for any citizen engagement toolbox. Elected officials want to be re-elected and developers must demonstrate they're effectively engaging the community-at-large to give them the social and political cover to approve the project without electoral backlash.

Every project has its unique aspects requiring none, some, or all the political marketing elements. For example, ballot box NIMBYism is not uncommon. Anti-development opponents circulate petitions gathering signatures to put the project on the ballot, thus, usurping the local elected body. Political marketing becomes front and center to not only win the support of elected officials, but now the majority of voters during early voting and Election Day.

VIDEO COMMUNICATIONS

The power of video communications cannot be overstated. Videos turn two-dimensional lifeless plans into three-dimensional realities. I'm not talking about jazzing up your sketches, but using video to humanize the project.

The face of the opposition is a voter, a homeowner, or a concerned citizen. They're full of emotion, passion, and conviction. Alternatively, the face of the project is rarely that of people. Typically, it's a thick three-ring binder, renderings, and high-priced consultants = advantage opposition.

The advantages of video are numerous, and I've asked Charles Belvin, a four-time Emmy winner to contribute his expertise in the upcoming chapter, *Lights, Camera, Action!*, to go more in-depth on the advantages of using video communications to humanize your projects to secure more approvals.

COMMUNITY BRIEFINGS

Town hall meetings and community workshops are often mandated in municipalities. So, if you must host a meeting, then ensure you have the homefield advantage. First, I recommend you call them community briefings, which connotate you are updating and reporting on the current status and merits of the project. Secondly, you don't have to offer just one big meeting that goes from 7-9 at night.

Instead, offer multiple time slots over the course of the day, evening and even week. For every time slot of let's say 60-90 minutes (12:00 to 1:30), you have a maximum of 10 to 15 attendees who must RSVP in advance. In the age of Covid, you're respecting the health and safety of the public, as well as minimizing the opposition's ability to blindside and overtake your venue.

Community briefings can be offered multiple days and time slots as well. Ensure you have your allies participate in these briefings. They're very effective in communicating the merits of the project to not only their fellow neighbors, but also the public officials who attend as well.

I haven't had one community briefing be hijacked by the opposition. It doesn't mean they haven't tried and tried again. In every case, they were outnumbered, and their hyperbole was ineffective.

SPEAKERS' BUREAU

Instead of inviting members of the community to attend one of your community briefings, be more proactive and engage civic and business groups offering yourself as a speaker/presenter.

Every community has some form of civic and business groups such as chamber, Rotary, Kiwanis, Elk or Lions Club and even the American Legion. Local community leaders participate in these organizations, and they aren't easily swayed by emotionally charged rhetoric, but driven by credible facts and logic. Moreover, they've probably heard about the project through the grapevine, so typically they accept your offer to speak for about 20 minutes or so.

It's never a waste of time to engage these influential members of the community with a presentation over breakfast or lunch. Also, these are membership-driven organizations, so the opposition is precluded from crashing the party to disrupt the forum. In the rare cases when they do crash, which I've witnessed firsthand, it doesn't go well for the opposition.

I had one client presenting to the local board of realtors. In the middle of the presentation to the board members, a literal knock came to the outside door. I answered and it was a reporter with a TV camera crew asking to interview (another hit job) the client. The chair of the board was so upset that the opposition tried to derail her meeting that she asked for a motion to support the hotel project.

We got a unanimous vote in support. I then went back out to the reporter who was still at the ready to attack offering not only my client, but the chairwoman hell bent to endorse the project. The news story turned from an attempted hit job to being a positive and persuasive story on the 6 o'clock news.

A=CE² GETS PROJECTS ACROSS THE FINISH LINE

In today's Digital Age, project approvals require more traditional and digital citizen engagement best practices. These practices are codified and carried out within and throughout integrated public affairs campaigns.

A=CE² gives you a comprehensive toolbox loaded with public affairs tools that can be modified and customized to fit the needs of projects. Some projects will need more crisis management to reduce the target, while other projects remain off the radar, so conducting grassroots engagement with influencers, while developing a project website would be more appropriate.

Fortunately, there's not a cookie cutter, one size fits all, model that can be deployed. I say fortunate, because the NIMBY Matrix™ feeds off of predictability and well-worn patterns of behavior.

This chapter was an introduction to the impact and influence of integrated public affairs guided by a simple equation based on proactive citizen engagement both in the real and virtual worlds.

The disconcerting question is which world is real? It's getting harder to tell one from the other.

LEVELING UP YOUR LEGAL GAME

Co-Contributing Author Brian Seymour, Esq.

I'm not a lawyer but recognize there isn't an effective integrated public affairs (IPA) campaign without legal counsel. The land-use lawyer is the four-star general who develops the legal strategies and political roadmaps for the proposed development project. Every project requires a legal "critical path" that maps out the process of approval. The best land-use lawyers understand the political gamesmanship that NIMBY opponents bring to the table, and the top-tier lawyers advise their clients to bring in a public relations, or preferably a public affairs professional.

Over the decades, I've worked with hundreds of land-use lawyers. In fact, more than half of my projects are the result of land-use lawyer referrals. When the lawyer and the public affairs operative are strategically and tactically on the same page, then the public affairs campaign is humming and putting the opposition on the defensive.

I asked Brian Seymour, Esq. to contribute his legal expertise to this chapter; offering his professional insights and experiences as it relates to getting controversial projects approved.

Brian co-chairs the real property practice of the Gunster Law Firm, with thirteen offices located throughout Florida. Operating from his West Palm Beach office, Brian is one of the go-to real estate and environmental lawyers for new development, redevelopment, and land use and zoning changes, often brought into the most impactful, complex, and often controversial development projects.

I've had the pleasure of working with Brian on several controversial projects.

SLEVIN: Brian for the benefit of our reader of this special chapter of *Breaking Out of the NIMBY* Matrix™, can you give a brief bio of yourself and the type of projects that you've worked on?

SEYMOUR: I am first and foremost an attorney. Although I am also a lobbyist for my projects, my viewpoint starts with legal requirements, process, and understanding of how these can shape project development and approvals. My goal is singular – how to obtain a viable development approval, and defend it if required, for my client.

I understand the political realities of what I do, and that just because something is legally permissible or approvable does not always mean it will get approved. If possible, I prefer to avoid litigation against governments because I know that it takes significant time and effort. However, with my background in land use and property rights litigation, I am always ready to take on that challenge if necessary.

In doing so, however, it is never personal – you will need to go back to that government for something in the future, so there is no need to burn bridges while you challenge them. In the approximately 25 years I have been practicing law, I have filed significant lawsuits when necessary and have used my understanding of the law and political realities to help obtain approvals for everything from gas stations to baseball stadiums, to horizontal and vertical mixed use developments – including the creation of a new City in Florida.

In doing so, I am also particularly proud to have been a part of the preservation of hundreds of thousands of acres of environmentally sensitive farmlands.

SLEVIN: Brian what makes for a good land-use lawyer in the real estate development space?

SEYMOUR: Those land-use lawyers who are at the top of their game exhibit a number of leadership characteristics for success, which I'll list out here:

- They have a proven record of securing approvals for complicated and controversial projects.
- They have successfully collaborated and optimized the skillsets of project planners, engineers, marketers, communicators, and various other consultants.
- They are considered active leaders in their communities; involved in various civic and business groups.

- They have close relationships with government staff, which offers great direct insights into the decision-making process.
- They have close relationships with most, if not all, of the elected officials.
- They have media interview skills that go beyond defaulting to "no comment."
- They understand the requirements – and more importantly limitations - of the notice and hearing system.
- They are savvy to the benefits of public affairs communications and grassroots lobbying.
- They are focused on securing project victories for their clients, understanding litigation should always be a last resort, but always ready to defend the approvals.
- They understand the impact that NIMBY opposition can have on their projects and when it is most likely to occur.

SLEVIN: Now that we know the minimum for what makes for a better than average land-use lawyer, what qualities differentiate top-tier lawyers from the slightly better than average?

SEYMOUR: The land-use lawyer is part of a team. It is critical to listen to everyone involved to find ways to solve problems. The legal process can be very helpful, and relationships with local government counsel to help them guide their clients is also critical. I see that there are three types of land use lawyers: (1) the pure lawyer, (2) the lobbyist, and (3) the hybrid – understanding both law and politics.

The best of us are the hybrid. Just knowing the law does not always get it done; maybe you can win a litigation, but it will take years and hundreds of thousands of dollars. Just focusing on the politics is also not enough; no matter how close you are to an elected, they have to listen to the voices of their constituents. A great land- use lawyer must be both – respected as a lawyer, known to care for the community not just lobbying for anything a client wants, and have good relationships.

It is also critical that the land-use lawyer know their limits: I am not a public affairs consultant, a pure lobbyist, a marketing professional, a planner, or an engineer. I need those professionals to make a project go. And, I need to get my ego out of the way and let whomever is right for the job do the job, regardless of what it is. Having a planner and engineer who can translate their pictures and analysis into something everyday people can understand it worth its weight in gold.

Having a public affairs strategist, communications professional, and sometimes even a pure lobbyist who may have key relationships is also preferrable. There is no one size fits all and following the same process every time does not work. That is the blue pill you talk about, Patrick, in your earlier chapters.

I have found that the red pill, the challenging of long held belief or standards, particularly in a fast changing technological world, is often the key to obtaining a project approval. Even if it means that the public never sees or hears from me. In all of this, it is also important for a lawyer to understand the legal basis for approvals.

Unfortunately, sometimes the approval is not the end. Litigation can ensue, some of it based only on the record of the approval hearings. If we do not have a proper record, the whole thing can come undone.

SLEVIN: How do you view the notice and hearing system?

SEYMOUR: I am a lawyer and I live in the communities in which I work. So, I understand that the notice and hearing system is important. It allows for constitutional process. That process, even when it might work against me, is the foundation of our entire society. So, I would not want to change it. That said, it is severely limiting. It is there for the public to be able to be a part of the process, to have their voice heard. But, it does not provide a complete picture.

I have seen people show up with 100 signatures on a petition, or worse with 100 people in a commission chamber. They have that right and should participate. But, those 100 people represent the tiniest fraction of the public. So, why should their voices be the only ones that matter when most people are fine with what we are doing. The sad truth is that people only show up when they are angry or upset. This skews the process.

So, to make it work honestly and effectively, it is important that we all find ways to have those who are supportive, who recognize the value in what we are bringing to the community, show up and have their voices heard as well. Though the legal process allows for that, in reality it does not encourage or support those voices.

This is the biggest limit – the process only provides a small sliver of the real story for those who are making the decision.

SLEVIN: When advising your clients, do you encourage the "flying under the radar" approach every time, sometimes, or rarely?

SEYMOUR: There is not a single answer. Sometimes, for smaller projects where there is unlikely to be challenges, "flying under the radar" can work. You don't want to raise issues unnecessarily. More and more, however, that is not likely. There are simply too many people right now who are the "I got mine and now it should stop" types. They got their 15-story condo when everything around it was two-story buildings. But, now that someone wants to do a 25-story building it is too much, it is incompatible, even though it is far more compatible than their building was.

The *reality* is that times are changing. We as communities need to grow or we will wither and die. But, change scares people. That is just human nature. So, more and more, we as development professionals need to get out ahead of the story, ahead of the fear.

We should be honest with ourselves and with the people in the community. If we are to add value, those who are against the project matter. Working with them from the start, bringing them to the table is never wrong. Even if they are intransigent and refuse to work with us, it will show the decision makers that they, the opponents, are not looking out for the community as a whole, but just for themselves.

SLEVIN: Your answer cues up the question on when to begin an integrated public affairs endeavor for the bigger or more controversial projects? As you're fully aware from our working together *The NIMBY Trifecta* of gossip and rumors circulate months before an application is formally filed. How do you communicate to your clients on when to pull the communications and engagement triggers?

SEYMOUR: This is an easy answer – NOW! What I mean by this is that when we have large scale projects, public affairs has to start as soon as we know we are moving forward. Large scale projects immediately create a fear factor in communities. What will it mean for traffic? Who will pay for infrastructure? Do we have enough first responders? Are our schools overcrowded already? How will it change my lifestyle? And many more concerns.

These can often be addressed but waiting until after the chatter starts, makes it much more difficult. This is also true for smaller projects that can still generate controversy. Getting out in front of an issue ultimately saves time, money, and gives us the best chance to obtain an approval.

SLEVIN: What have your observed about today's NIMBY opposition compared to say 10-15 years ago? How much has social media (websites, Facebook, apps, emails, blogs) changed the rules of citizen engagement?

SEYMOUR: There are two main issues with NIMBY today. The first is economics. During the Great Recession, people understood the value of development and redevelopment. As the economy has strengthened, people have changed their positions, as have elected officials. This gives people more power to say no and a key value to development and redevelopment is not persuasive, meaning that we need to have different messages and messengers.

The second is technology. It is far too easy for a few to spread misinformation and fear to their neighbors and the community-at-large; this also helps to create media frenzy with easy click bait for online views. The use of Facebook groups (such as "engage" groups), neighborhood apps (such as *Nextdoor*), and blogs allow for the few to influence the many with misinformation and fear mongering without factual basis. Once these negative emotional responses are inculcated into the neighborhood psyche, real facts and positive impacts end up being irrelevant.

Trying to change minds is much more difficult than it is to create positive impact upfront. This is even more difficult with the ability of the NIMBY to constantly inundate its message with virtually no cost and without any oversight or counterforce.

Even when traditional media takes a particular view, there are editors, other writers, and a need for revenue that can impact their reporting. None of this exists without social media, apps, blogs and the like, all of which build on themselves to constantly churn the same negative messaging.

Finally, no matter what, the community is not going to listen to the counter facts from the developer and its team – they are seen as biased and not to be trusted. So, it is more important than ever to have advocates among the community.

SLEVIN: Brian as you know citizen engagement consists of elements of grassroots lobbying and advocacy. Do you think third-party letters, phone calls, emails, face-to-face intercepts, and speaking at hearings is vital to overcoming the NIMBY factor?

SEYMOUR: I have referred to this in other contexts as third-party validation. It is critical. No matter how right we are as the developer's team – the planning, the engineering, etc. being well thought out and providing value for a community – it is too easy to discount us because we are "hired guns." Having others who see the benefits, who understand the value and the details of the project, allows us to come together to counter the NIMBY. The more we have people saying yes, we have a chance to overcome the people who say no.

SLEVIN: Agreed. It's not what you say as the applicant, but who says it for you! How do you account for the local news media? What do you advise your clients regarding potential media engagement? What materials do you or your public affairs team members put together for them if anything?

SEYMOUR: Traditional reporters and editors may try to be unbiased, but they are human beings. They are influenced by the same things as the rest of us, their experiences and too often the loudest and most negative voices. They also unfortunately in today's world have a mixed agenda – selling papers and reporting.

Of course, not every member of the local media is the same. So, like everything else, the answer to when and how to engage the media depends on the project and issues. However, having good relationships with the local media helps. Knowing them, and being trusted by them, can help a story.

It is also extremely helpful to have advocates among the community, those who understand that development does not have to be bad and that there are many positives that can come with it. From that, having discussions with the media, the developer, the planner, the attorney, and/or community advocates with the appropriate information can be extremely useful.

Without that, having information available on a website, project information to provide the media, doing Q&As, or interviews is not as effective. Without trust, all the information in the world is too easy to ignore. With that, the media can be extremely useful in providing a balanced message, if you can get to them before they hear from the NIMBYs and have already made up their mind.

SLEVIN: What have you seen from real estate industries and associations with respect to best practices to neutralize NIMBYism in the digital space? Can you cite any seminars, studies, reports, white papers?

SEYMOUR: Very little exists in this arena. We tend to go with what we know. I admit that I am not one who attends many seminars and reads industry advice on the subject. I have seen firsthand what can work and I know folks, like you, with the knowledge to engage the community for positive impact. The more success is had, the more likely that the stories get out and more of this will occur. But, mostly, we learn what has been done and tend to follow that path. It is human nature.

SLEVIN: How does integrated public affairs change the political landscape?

SEYMOUR: I have not seen anything more effective than IPA. By getting out in front of large scale, complex and difficult development issues, IPA can create a positive before the negative comes out. And, when you have the positive mindset to start, when you have advocates who are voters and community leaders – not just business leaders, but neighbors who will gain from the development – you can create the political atmosphere that can help you obtain approvals.

SLEVIN: Unfortunately, we see NIMBY activism spill over into litigation. You've won the approval battle at the municipal level, but could lose the war in court. How important is litigation communications when it comes to promoting the merits of the project and reputation management for your client?

SEYMOUR: This is one of the most delicate balancing acts we have. It is what separates the good from the great. Lawyers too often get locked into trying to craft a perfect legal message. Lobbyists get too locked into trying to craft the perfect political message. In the first, you can go so far that the lawyer for the government (or the NIMBY) gets put on notice and either creates counter evidence or makes everyone lose trust in anything else said about the project – they think they are getting set up.

In the second, you may not have the evidence you need to defend an approval, or challenge a denial, or worse you create evidence that can hurt you in litigation. I started my career solely in litigation, defending approvals and challenging denials, in administrative proceedings as well as in state and federal courts. Too often, the law is stacked against the landowner and developer. If we are not careful during the approval process – both before and during the hearings – it can become that much more difficult.

SLEVIN: What are the pros and cons to recommending a local public affairs professional who has the political, communications and grassroots advocacy capabilities to protect the legal critical path?

SEYMOUR: This is a tough question. Obviously, the pros are that a good local professional knows the community, and they often know the politics. The downside, however, can be that they may have people in the community that do not like them or worse do not trust them. Unlike a lawyer where we are often decried simply due to our profession (this is why I often stay away from the direct public engagement, keeping behind the scenes), the public affairs consultant needs to be able to bring people together.

You must be able to gain trust. There is also a risk that if a public affairs consultant does not understand some of the legal issues that arise during the course of a challenging process, they may say things that can hurt our legal strategy. This has to be balanced. Working with someone who has experience in this specific arena and who knows how to work with a land use team is critical.

Sometimes that means working with a local and an outside specialist, like you, or just conveniently bringing someone like you into the community. I have seen you learn a community incredibly quickly and gain support that I didn't think was possible. Not being local helped with that because you were a fresh face without any preconceptions by the community, empowering us to win social and political support.

SLEVIN: Brian, no doubt those land-development professionals who remain blue pilled give you a competitive advantage when it comes to navigating the legal and political realities in an ever-changing world. Do you have any advice for those who have decided to pursue the red pill road less traveled pathway?

SEYMOUR: My parting thought is this - call Patrick Slevin early in your process. I know this is your book. That is not why I say it. What I have seen you do is remarkable and working with you is a great education. The proof is in the experience. Once you work with a great IPA team, the more you will want to.

Moreover, don't be afraid of the extra help, even if it means less money for you in the short run. As a land-use lawyer, I know my community and my local politics. But, that does not mean that there are not times when we need to add someone like you to our team. Success on projects and happy clients are the best business development one can do and when you put clients first – which is what this is about, that is always the best choice.

I also think that sharing these ideas wherever possible – providing copies of this book, speaking about the positive experience with the red pill at industry groups such as ULI, NAIOP, ICSC, etc. -, is good. I think that the more people know about the value of the red pill – using IPA in the right circumstances – the better off all of us in the industry will be, clients and consultants. I am happy to have others join me in this. A rising tide raises all boats... and a really good land-use lawyer will still be needed.

SLEVIN: I greatly appreciate your endorsement and validation of the work. The reality is, I cannot work on every project, which is why I wrote the book, to truly help our colleagues in the industry break out of the NIMBY Matrix™ to gain more success. However, a book in of itself is not enough to accomplish this mission, which is why I have the Academy of Citizen Engagement (www.AceMyAudience.com) providing elite-level knowledge, experience, and services.

As an expert who provides his legal insights to the Academy's clientele, what do you care to add?

SEYMOUR: I think having a citizen engagement organization like A.C.E. that's completely focused on educating and arming corporate leaders and professionals for the public square is long overdue. As a lifelong proponent of better citizen participation, I'm proud to offer my legal experience to such an esteemed assembly of VIPs.

I applaud your making A.C.E. an exclusive, limited membership, catering to a resolute community of leaders and professionals who understand they must effectively inform and influence the audiences that affect their bottom lines. Everyone else is focused on quantity, while A.C.E. is focused on top-shelf quality of programing and services. This also allows real engagement, just like we do when countering the NIMBYs, that provides extra value that you can't get at a large seminar.

This is exciting and I've recommended A.C.E. to several clients and colleagues to sign up for the waiting list. Hopefully, I have some sway with getting them in, given we've known each other for a few decades.

SLEVIN: Of course, Brian. A referral from you goes a long way. There's more on A.C.E. in the closing chapter. Brian, thank you for sharing your expertise and contributing the value of the book. I appreciate it. Where can readers find you, should they have any legal questions?

SEYMOUR: My pleasure, Patrick. They can find me at www.Gunster.com. You can just type my name in the search bar at the top right.

DIGITAL AWARENESS IN A NIMBY WORLD

Co-Contributing Author Jennings DePriest

On any given day, there are hundreds of anti-development groups attacking projects with Facebook, online petition drives, websites, blogs, vlogs (video blogs), YouTube, and a host of other digital platforms.

For many corporate real estate developers and land-use professionals, the digital space is a foreign country with a foreign language. Alternatively, real estate development opponents have enjoyed immense success monopolizing the digital space and putting developers on the defensive.

I've asked digital marketing expert Jennings DePriest to contribute to this chapter. Jennings brings not only digital expertise and know-how, but he has excelled in public affairs and political digital marketing. We've worked together on NIMBY-related projects producing outstanding results in countering and neutralizing digital-NIMBY activism.

SLEVIN: Let's jump in. Is reality getting harder to discern with the advent of social media and the advances of virtual reality?

DEPRIEST: Unequivocally yes, but the bigger issue is that there is truly less of a difference between "reality" and virtual reality in the modern world.

If an inaccurate Tweet gets 2.4 million views and the retraction only gets 2,400 views, which has more of an impact on the real world?

If a teenager spends the majority of their waking hours playing video games, what is more real to them, the video game, or "real" life?

Research shows that the human brain has a hard time telling the difference between an imagined experience and actual reality. How much more real will the brain view hyper-realistic imagery tied to regular dopamine hits?

There are countless studies and anecdotal reports of pornography users becoming unable to have real sex because for them, porn is real sex.

Looking at Maslov's Hierarchy of Needs, the average American who has time to spend online already has their physiological needs met, and in some cases, may have their safety needs met more adequately by staying online instead of venturing out into the crime riddled streets.

SLEVIN: Okay with that context, what is digital media and marketing? We assume we know, but maybe there's more to it than meets the layman's eye?

DEPRIEST: Digital marketing is really just a catch all for modern communication and marketing strategies. It basically encompasses every medium that wasn't available for marketing and communications firms prior to Al Gore infamously stating he invented the internet.

When people hear "digital marketing" they think "social media marketing" and stop there, even more detrimental, they think "Facebook marketing" and exclude social media platforms like YouTube. Digital marketing works best when you take a look at the whole picture of what's possible and then narrow your strategy from there.

SLEVIN: Before we get into strategies, can you give us a better picture of the digital users?

DEPRIEST: What may surprise most people is the fact that 72 percent or nearly three out of four Americans use social media, while seven percent of Americans don't use the internet at all. The most significant factor in use of digital media is high school graduation status. People who did not graduate high school are 12 percent less likely to use social media or the internet than their diploma holding counterparts.

Going back into the idea of leveraging the whole digital ecosystem, while only 72 percent of Americans use social media, 81 percent of Americans use text messaging regularly.

SLEVIN: What are the top three sites today?

DEPRIEST: The top three websites are Google (13.53B daily visits), YouTube (7.65B daily visits), and Facebook (4.18B daily visits). It is worth noting that many people have Google set as their default homepage on their computer (the same reason MicrosoftOnline.com comes in 17th for traffic with 455.03M visits).

SLEVIN: What's the attention span of folks in the digital world? What's the dangers and what are the opportunities, if any?

DEPRIEST: The impact of digital media on all aspects of mental health, including attention span is terrifying. With the rise of TikTok and its competitors (Instagram and Facebook Reels, YouTube Shorts) the American attention span is dropping lower than ever before, particularly across younger demographics.

It's a sad trend that across all mediums most Americans cannot read and comprehend more than three lines of text at a time.

Not sentences, lines!

That means that marketers must be cognizant of the way text will appear in any medium they are leveraging to get their message across and adjust accordingly. The average attention span of an American adult was 12.5 seconds in 2000. That number is 8.25 seconds today.

SLEVIN: Armed with this digital awareness, what opportunities present themselves to professionals looking to educate and influence audiences in this digital reality?

DEPRIEST: The major opportunity is leveraging videos to communicate instead of text (59 percent of senior executives prefer to watch a video than read text if they had the choice), but even that poses some risks.

Eighty five percent of online videos are viewed silently, so subtitling videos is essential for success, but again, this gets back to the reading comprehension of the voter. When in doubt, smaller words, and prettier colors.

SLEVIN: How are political campaigns capitalizing on the use of content and where are they posting?

DEPRIEST: Unless you're running for 8th grade class president, political campaigns should start and end with Facebook.

Because of its demographics and content style, Facebook is the home of undecided voters who actually vote. It also serves as a more geographically localized platform for messaging, meaning your constituency will actually be seen.

Twitter is an incredible platform for engaging with voters in a more personal way, but it's the platform of super voters. Twitter users are highly segmented into atmospheres (hence "money twitter", "black twitter", etc.) and RARELY do not have their minds made up on those topics. Twitter also eschews geographic boundaries, so for anything short of a federal campaign, you are just spinning your wheels.

SLEVIN: In my opinion, too many people turn into an avatar when they're on social media. Seems they get caught up in their own created persona. I've certainly seen the NIMBY crowd getting caught up in their own found celebrity.

DEPRIEST: People in general are an avatar of their own beliefs and they strive for consistency. Social media makes this problem exponentially worse because it increases the social pressure for consistency.

People in the physical world naturally move to neighborhoods of others who share their values, so they naturally only have exposure to people within a few political, social, and intellectual degrees of variance from themselves. This self-polices a certain level of moderation in views, save for a few exceptions with particularly charismatic leaders.

On the internet however, you can quickly go down a rabbit hole of increasingly radical information that calls for increasingly radical consistency in beliefs. In right-wing communities, this is commonly called "taking the red pill" though the situation is truly universal, happening on both sides of the aisle.

Within NIMBY campaigns, it is even easier for people to become obsessed with their avatar and go deeper and deeper down the rabbit hole because they are experiencing local celebrity and leadership, which is often devoid of the general social pressure of the entirety of the internet mob.

SLEVIN: How important is digital communications to the integrated public affairs approach to overcoming and neutralizing NIMBY opposition?

DEPRIEST: Countering digital activism with digital citizen engagement is essential for overcoming and neutralizing NIMBY opposition, but it has to look and feel homegrown and local.

If you're using peer-to-peer texting, you should try to have videos from local residents to send to potential supporters.

If you're building a website, you must protect the domain registration and make sure it is something a high school student with a decent understanding of WordPress could build.

If you're using Facebook groups, you should promote community leaders to be the administrators.

The fact of the matter is that digital media feeds traditional media in an endless cycle.

If you are not taking advantage of the massive impact this can have on your ability to influence policy makers and the masses, you are missing out.

SLEVIN: What's your take on NIMBY opposition campaigns on Facebook and other social media sites? Are they effective? Do they facilitate viral impressions? Do they help build coalitions? Is it more façade or true substance? In other words, if you do nothing to counter the dawn of digital NIMBY activism, what are the consequences?

DEPRIEST: Fortunately for developers, most NIMBY campaigns on Facebook (and more recently, *NextDoor*) are poorly run operations that are headed up by a few squeaky wheels.

Unfortunately, those squeaky wheels make a lot of noise on decision makers' pages and therefore end up getting a lot of grease.

Word-of-mouth is rare in NIMBY campaigns, because if it isn't in someone's backyard, they probably don't care.

This can be used to the advantage of developers, because they can often tap into a larger audience of people who do care.

For instance, a small set of residents may not like that a grocery store is being built in front of their neighborhood – BUT residents in surrounding neighborhoods might LOVE the idea of having closer groceries.

In many cases, developers can expand the audience of people who will benefit from development more easily than the NIMBY crowd can find more people who have perceived negative consequences.

Developers who are able to think strategically about NIMBY opposition have the upper hand, if they are willing to use it.

SLEVIN: Let me stop you there. You previously mentioned developing a project website and a pro-project Facebook group. Most of the professionals are not that familiar with these basic digital elements that will help them succeed in the NIMBY Matrix™. Can you explain why these two digital/social components so important to winning approval?

DEPRIEST: When the grapevine begins spreading its gossip, and people begin to learn about the project or the developer, what are they going to do? They're going to Google search the developer, the company, and/or the project. If there isn't any information in the top 3-5 links on Google on the company, then it screams untrustworthy and lacking credibility.

Facebook is one of the cornerstones of today's digital activism. Anti-development groups have become adept at spreading their allegations, attacks, and misinformation effectively – not just with the immediate project, but throughout a growing network of similar anti-development Facebook groups and activists.

The developers who have taken the red pill are finding success by establishing their own Facebook project group pages.

Facebook is great for engagement, but the true centerpiece of the campaign should be a landing page that communicates the benefits of the project. The landing page is a one-way communication tool, so it is easier to maintain (because NIMBY people can't post nasty comments).

If you text out the landing page as part of a public opinion survey, you're already ahead in the battle.

SLEVIN: How influential is digital media when it comes to public officials making decisions? Please explain how they are influenced by Facebook and other digital activism.

DEPRIEST: Public officials are really looking for cover and capital more than anything when it comes to taking votes that might make the NIMBY crowd mad.

By growing a campaign on social media or driving people to sign a virtual petition on a landing page, you're giving public officials the cover they need to take your side.

Imagine being able to walk to the podium at a meeting with a box of 500+ digitally signed petitions in your hand.

It makes it *much* easier for the public official to feel like they are siding with the people, not simply siding with the money.

SLEVIN: How important is citizen engagement in the digital space? What's your opinion on best practices of engaging local stakeholders to achieve project approvals?

DEPRIEST: Citizen engagement is the key to long term success in the digital space – especially for developers who focus on key regions. One of the key things I focus on when speaking to members at the Academy of Citizen Engagement is their ability to grow a movement over time that can be activated on every project in an area.

Without true citizen buy-in, you may be able to win one or two campaigns, but after that – you'll be burned and outed as an "astroturfer" (a manufactured corporate campaign with no citizen support)

SLEVIN: I appreciate you offering your professional insights. How can people find you and your firm?

DEPRIEST: You can find me on Twitter, Instagram, and LinkedIn @JenningsLawton, or you can visit my company's website at www.TopLobster.com.

LIGHTS, CAMERA, ACTION

Co-Contributing Author Charles Belvin

Ever since Thomas Edison invented film in the late 1800's and the Lumiere Brothers invented the projector it became immediately evident that "motion pictures" had the power not only to tell a story but evoke emotions on the part of the viewer. In fact, it was only a few years later during the Spanish American War when we began to see propaganda films appear which were produced for that very purpose (influencing public opinion) and they have been produced non-stop, ever since, by all sides in every conflict.

VIDEO EVOKES EMOTIONS

Film, (and in today's world, video), has the power to evoke powerful emotions in the viewer and most people use emotions as a guide in decision making. As Carl W. Buehner said..."*They may forget what you said — but they will never forget how you made them feel*'.

The printed word has limited power to accomplish this. Think about it... when you read an article or even a good book, you "hear" the voice in your head doing the narration...but it's usually your own voice you hear...you are reading it to yourself. This voice in your head may or may not be emotionally charged when you come across certain passages or dialogue.

But when you watch something on video or film, you are witnessing another person's expression of that same information...their tone of voice, the look in their eyes, the passion of their delivery...and if it's done well or done with a significant emotional charge, you can't help but "feel" it. And that feeling has a significant impact on decisions you make.

VIDEO IS PREFERRED OVER PRINTED COPY

Numerous studies show that when a person is offered an article to read or a video to watch, nine times out of ten, they will go for the video over the printed word. No wonder Google spent billions of dollars to purchase YOUTUBE. Videos let you tell a story, which reaches out and connects with people and shows them who you are and what your message is and what your brand is all about. Consequently, a video reaches more people than an article. Moreover, you can upload a video to any website which makes creating brand awareness even easier.

And by the way, it's available 24 hours a day, seven days a week.

VIDEO FOSTERS WORD-OF-MOUTH

Ask anyone over the age of 50 to name one major attribute of Volvo automobiles and nine times out of ten, they will say "safety". Next, ask them how many Volvos they owned, and most will say "none".

This begs the question; how do they know they're safe? It is likely they will not know how they got this information...it's just something that "everyone knows".

The back story is that in the 60's, Volvo ran a series of commercials showing their automobiles being subjected to crash tests with the message that while other companies are focused on speed or style, Volvo is focused on safety. The message not only stuck, but to this day, it is still passed around by word of mouth. Volvos are safe...everyone knows that.

VIDEO ALLOWS YOU TO CRAFT THE MESSAGE YOUR WAY

Many of you have probably given a speech or made a presentation of some sort. Did you use a power-point? If you did, it's probably because you wanted to show the information conveyed in a concise and logical manner and hopefully, it was easily understood by the viewers. The important word here is "show"...you wanted to show them the information. You could have simply read something to them or explained it verbally, but showing an image or picture helps get the message across.

Now imagine trying to coordinate your presentation, verbally and visually, with a live music track. Make sure your delivery matches the timing and nuances of the music. Good so far?

How about lighting...did you make arrangements to create a certain mood in the room? Are you standing on the stage in a room lit with overhead fluorescent "house lights" or are does your presentation look like a TED talk? Again, the key word here is "look", i.e., what does it look like?

Just to explore this point a little further...psychologists know that it is virtually impossible to avoid picturing in your mind a pink giraffe with purple polka dots if I tell you not to.

Don't do it...whoops! Too late.

We think...and most importantly we remember...things in visual terms. This is why pneumonic memory techniques universally utilize pictures and images to improve memory retention.

A professionally produced video allows you to craft a script and get the words exactly as you want them and delivered with a voice that matches the feeling you are looking for. Or your video may incorporate soundbites that were carved out of an interview and selected specifically for your message. Add music, good lighting, informational graphics, etc., and you have a presentation that is delivered to your audience in the best way possible, again, 24/7.

VIDEO HUMANIZES THE PROJECT

For this topic, let's take a proposed solar farm for example. What characteristics of a 5000-acre solar farm will have the greatest appeal to the residents who live near it? Pick one...

1. The project will look very "state of the art" and will have a security fence around it.
2. The project is endorsed and supported by your local state officials.
3. The project will create 200 jobs to the area and the farmers who sign a 30-year lease of their property will receive reliable income regardless of weather conditions and help save their farms from financial ruin.

Hmmmm...let me see. Which one?

Obviously, to the residents who live in the area, even if they are not the ones who live literally right next to the project, choice number 3 will carry the most weight when it comes to a vote. It is very likely they empathize with their neighbors and would like to see them avoid failure even if a solar farm does not make for a pastoral landscape.

So how do we get this message out there? Certainly, you could produce a slick video with a celebrity host and special effects...but I think hearing directly from the neighbors that are directly affected will have a greater impact. Especially if they are known...and trusted.

So how do we get you to experience the neighbor's perspective? We interview them in a video. We tell their stories. We discover they're doing it because it will help offset the ups and downs inherent in farming and help them keep from going bankrupt due to unexpected severe weather.

Did you know that solar panels can eventually be removed from the property and the land can be put back to producing crops? How do I know this?...I watched the video.

If you ever get the chance, google the "IKEA Lamp Commercial" produced by Spike Jonze. In this spot, a girl bought a new lamp for her apartment and has decided to throw the old lamp out. She puts it on the street for garbage truck to pick up. Underneath all of this is sad music that makes us feel that the old lamp is being rejected. Discarded. Tossed aside. Homeless. We see it sitting on the sidewalk at night... in the rain... while the "new" lamp is warm and cozy next to the girl's easy chair in the apartment. More sad music... Poor, poor lamp.

Then the music stops, and a man walks in front of the camera and says, "You have feelings for this lamp but that's because you are crazy. This lamp has no feelings. It's just a lamp. Besides...the new lamp is much better. Get over it."

All of a sudden, we realize he's right. The way the story was presented...the music...the way it was shot...the angles and lighting...all evoked an emotional response to an electrical appliance that has no emotions whatsoever.

Sounds to me like a great way to address a NIMBY issue.

CONCLUDING REMARKS BY PATRICK SLEVIN

Charlie, thank you, for laying out in this chapter the value and impact of video communications. The key takeaway in countering and overcoming the gnashing of teeth of NIMBYism is by humanizing or putting a face on the project. Not every project has an emotional story to sell, but it's worth the circumspection to find the potential story that may be hiding in plain sight.

The power of video communications cannot be overstated. Something as simple as a video testimonial from the developer or corporate officer talking about their commitment to the community-at-large and being dedicated good neighbors is better than a written biography. We want to see the sincerity and body language that gives meaning to the words. Otherwise, it's two-dimensional, unimaginative communications that are straining to reach and resonate with targeted audiences.

Ideally, you're securing video endorsements and testimonials from local leaders: Former officials, business and civic leaders, small-business owners, contractors, and anyone who has local connections to the community.

If you cannot secure any testimonials supporting the current project, then you can produce video endorsements and testimonials from previous stakeholders who had a great experience in working with you and your past projects.

Charlie and I have worked together on many projects spanning nearly two decades. I've learned a lot from him. Most importantly, video communications isn't the about equipment, but being able to tell your story in a digital format.

Corporate developers have great stories to share in the public square, and it's an unutilized tool that can be a game changer, if promoted up to the top of your toolbox.

To learn more about Charlie Belvin go to his website at www.CharlesBelvin.com

FIST IN A VELVET GLOVE

In my Spring 2019 article, A Silver Linings Playbook for Controversial Development Projects, published in *Development Magazine* put out by NAIOP, I asked who would oppose a new Hospital? Typically, it wasn't the local neighbors, but competitors protecting their market share.

However, these so-called "hospital wars" started to see more and more homeowners jumping into the fray of NIMBYism. That article was a precursor to writing this chapter for the book. Developers can secure corporate and community goodwill by operating assertively, but sensitively in the public square.

The key to the article and this chapter is understanding that the opposition's political gamesmanship (organic and professional) must be met with equal or greater hardball. This doesn't mean you're endangering your corporate reputation and image, but rather, you're leveraging and asserting it to your advantage.

HARDBALL THUGGERY

There's an unspoken rule of "take no prisoners" in the NIMBY Matrix™. NIMBY opponents play political hardball when attacking projects, companies, and people. They don't hold back their anger and angst, and sometimes good people get hurt beyond the political rhetoric.

It's not pretty. I've literally seen commissioners shaking in fear due to rumored threats of "red-neck justice" with a potential .30-06 round greeting them when they get their mail at the end of their dirt driveways. In another project, I witnessed a mob standing outside a county courthouse threatening to hang a black elected official, while displaying a noose. I've had activists travel from another state trying to get into my neighborhood looking for my home, but fortunately, I lived in a gated community at the time.

This is why I've operated under the radar on projects and kept my developer clients, past and present, confidential. It's part of the reason why small circle land-development professionals know of me in this space. I'm retained to operate much like a Navy Seal, parachuting into projects across the nation, covertly working behind the scenes empowering the client, consultants, and allies. My profile has been so low that often I sit among the opposition in public hearings, reporting to the client what is coming up to the podium.

Political gamesmanship is the order of the day. People can get hurt, and it can elevate quickly beyond what is reasonable for public discourse. Ironically, NIMBY opponents demand corporate developers show transparency, goodwill, and concessions, while playing their double-standard of hardball thuggery.

This is why I recommend and operate with a fist in a velvet glove approach.

THE VELVET GLOVE

The community-at-large grants the license to operate, which means the applicant must earn the community's support for the project. The community elects their representatives and entrusts them to exercise due diligence before issuing or denying said license to operate. This comes in the form of a majority vote that is influenced by public discourse playing out in the public square.

Therefore, a company, for it to earn a majority approval for its development application(s), must be reputable, credible, and a good corporate neighbor, as well as submitting a well-planned project proposal.

Company leaders, executives, developers, and their land-development consultants must present themselves as good neighbors trying to rally the community around the project and be seen as consensus builders. The optics must be positive, inspiring, and deliberate.

This is what I call the velvet glove. Instead of being seen as reactive to hostile forces and being defensive, the velvet glove conveys the impressions of respecting the community-at-large. It doesn't go into tunnel vision reacting to crisis, but rather, recognizing the public square is broader and public discourse must remain civil.

It never bodes well for the developer to appear argumentative with the opposition in public hearings or in news stories.

Companies that embrace and execute traditional and digital forms of citizen engagement ($A=CE^2$ equation) consistently convey the velvet glove that garners corporate and community goodwill.

These are external impressions vital to securing political approvals. I cannot stress it enough; developers cannot be seen fighting or antagonizing the constituents of elected officials. This is contrary to the tenets of public discourse, as well as breaching corporate governance and socially responsible investment factors such as E.S.G. (environmental, social, and governance).

However, a velvet glove alone won't secure greater success.

FIST IN THE VELVET GLOVE

Integrated public affairs accomplishes the velvet glove objectives of generating corporate goodwill impressions. It's proactive, responsive, and deliberate in *minimizing* the target on your back during a crisis, while *maximizing* your corporate reputation. Integrated public affairs is actively engaging citizens to pre-empt NIMBY attacks and turning them into a positive posture in the public square.

The velvet glove is for external audiences as previously mentioned. The fist that goes into the velvet glove is integrated public affairs as well, but for achieving internal objectives.

Again, the politics of real estate is a blood sport, and NIMBY opponents are adept at political hardball. So, how does a corporate good neighbor conduct itself in this kill or be killed political thunderdome?

The purpose of the fist is to *marginalize* the NIMBY opposition. The beauty of it is this: You're feeding the NIMBY opposition the rope to hang themselves vis-à-vis they lose their credibility in the public square.

Stay with me.

Your integrated public affairs campaign is a fist in a velvet glove duality. While you're generating positive, external optics of truly engaging citizens, you're also eroding away the opposition's stage, giving them less opportunities for stoking conflict. This indirect, but purposeful posture forces the opposition into a corner.

As you're building consensus, recruiting advocates and surrogates, placing positive news and social media stories, and securing the political high ground, you're indirectly, but purposely feeding the opposition the rope that hangs them – politically speaking.

You're helping them *marginalize* themselves before public officials, reporters, and community-at-large. When you take away their ability to foster conflict, coupled with your integrated public affairs elements, opponents are put on the defensive; they go off message and feel compelled to attack anyone or anything.

They predictably become old hat where their attacks became more belligerent, while their rhetoric becomes fatigued and less effective. Reporters are not so keen on running their stories or quoting them as prominently, if at all.

In short order, public officials begin to sense the political tides shifting. Your allies become emboldened, and folks sitting on the fence gain more confidence to publicly support the project.

It doesn't take much for the fist in the velvet glove to garner corporate goodwill, while helping the opposition to *marginalize* themselves. The beauty of it is everything is consistent with the rules of citizen engagement in the public square.

If you want to learn about my Triple-M Strategies of *Minimize*, *Maximize,* and *Marginalize*, you can read more in detail in my first book, Never Lose to NIMBY Opposition Again!; Master the Secrets, Strategies, and Solutions for Turning NIMBY Crisis Into Your Finest Hour.

CITIZEN PARTICIPATION REPORTS

Your citizen engagement activities are above board, facilitating constructive dialogue, educating stakeholders, and responsive to audiences that impact your bottom-line interests. This is much more preferrable to the "flying under the radar" posture of reacting to NIMBY attacks, abdicating the strategic high ground, and losing control over the fate of your projects.

The fist in a velvet glove is a strong and pragmatic approach to the realities dictated in the NIMBY Matrix™.

When it comes time for the application to be submitted, I recommend you submit for public consumption what I call a Citizen Engagement Report. In this report, you summarize and itemize every person you have interfaced and engaged. It can be added to the application.

The report will include dates, locations, and names derived from a bevy of citizen engagement activities:

- Neighborhood coffees
- Door knocking
- Speaking before the Rotary
- Direct mailers
- Handouts (Fact Sheets, FAQ, Bios)
- Community briefings
- Letter inviting neighbors to community briefings with mailing list
- Emails and phone calls you answered
- Project website
- Texting campaigns

- Print and radio ads
- Facebook groups
- Reporter briefings
- Video and written testimonials
- Copies of emails supporting the project sent to elected officials
- Pro-project signatures (petitions)
- Opinion poll
- Guest columns
- Letters to the editor
- Letters to opposition responding to their allegations
- Press releases and statements
- Positive and maybe fair news articles in the mix

I think you get the idea of the volume of positive impressions you can package for public officials, the news media, and the community-at-large with a Citizen Participation Report. If you're able to demonstrate that you've done more than just react to the opposition's dictations, then you've helped community decision makers look beyond the sub-set of citizens who have a self-serving interest.

As the public hearings draw near, you can submit supplemental Citizen Engagement Reports to demonstrate not only ongoing interaction in the public square, but any compromises and concessions derived from listening to other opinions.

Believe me when I say, elected officials love seeing the developer actively trying to mitigate *reasonable* concerns in the community.

The fist in the velvet glove is effective and ensures you will govern your integrated public affairs from the strategic high ground – every blessed time.

EARLY BIRD GETS THE WORM

The best NIMBY crisis is the one that never happens and engaging the community earlier gives you a better model for success. We now know NIMBY risks and conflicts can be mitigated in the absence of conventional thinking. The key to success often begins with the question on when to start your integrated public affairs operations.

This is the most asked question I get from clients, colleagues, and audiences. My answer is always the same, “It depends on the dynamics of the community, the project, the company, the development team, and the industry.”

There isn’t a cookie cutter template strategy that can be seamlessly applied to every situation, but there are public affairs best practices that can be called upon to help you decide on when to launch your citizen engagement operations and what tools you should deploy as you move forward.

BEGIN ATTACKING THE NIMBY TRIFECTA

As you read previously, the NIMBY trifecta is comprised of community gossip spread by the grapevine, which is then validated by the archaic notice and hearing process, which is finally emboldened by the passive posture of "flying under the radar." These patterns reverberate countless times in the NIMBY Matrix™ universe.

Armed with this knowledge, you can begin to map out an integrated public affairs strategy and campaign. You begin by asking yourself when you think the rumors will start to circulate about the property or project. This could be as far out as year or more, or three to six months before the application is formally filed.

The objective is to stay ahead of the gossip by pre-empting and possibly deconstructing it before it takes on a life of its own. Alternatively, you may see an opportunity to create buzz for your project that usurps any misinformation campaigns. The latter is only advisable if you see the opportunity to quickly claim the strategic high ground and operate from it consistently throughout the approval process. It's very gratifying to see this scenario play out.

Before you take any external action, you must get your arms around the community dynamics and appreciate what makes it tick. Due diligence is the key to early and ongoing success.

DO YOUR DUE DILIGENCE

More than 2000 years ago Chinese general and military strategist Sun Tzu wrote one of the greatest books ever written on military strategy and tactics titled, *The Art of War*.

He offered great advice on how to win a war, "If you know your enemy and know yourself, you need not fear the results of a hundred battles."

In the NIMBY Matrix™, less than one (1) percent of developers conduct social assessments of the communities where they seek to secure the license to operate. The number nearly reaches zero when you factor in their own lack of self awareness. This means that more than 99 percent of developers rarely know their opposition, but more importantly, they operate with corporate silos that prevent them from overcoming their own internal flaws and liabilities.

To paraphrase Sun Tzu, "If you don't know who your enemy is, then you'll lose half the battles...if you don't know who you are and you don't know your enemy, then you'll lose a hundred battles."

Every integrated public affairs operation is rooted in strategic planning that's underwritten by community, opposition, political, and corporate due diligence. If you invest just a portion of your resources and time into the below due diligence protocols, then you'll indeed be an early bird who not only gets the worm, but gain an advantage over would-be NIMBY forces as you get closer to filing your application.

COMMUNITY DUE DILIGENCE

Every community is different, but every community is the same. True, there's a big difference between urban, suburban, and rural communities, which I trust speaks for itself. However, what makes them the same are several aspects worth assessing to ensure greater success in the public square.

The character of the community and its perceived quality of life are staples of concern in every community profile. Every community has its share of opinion leaders at the intersections of influence looking out for the character of their communities. Part of the community due diligence is finding out who these community leaders may be. Note: a good start to getting intel is by asking your local land-use lawyer or planner, which they'll know a few.

However, the best way to find opinion leaders a.k.a. influentials is by asking the elected officials themselves. Often, they'll refer you to influential members of the community who act as their kitchen cabinet advisors.

Other opinion leaders could be the past or present president of the local chamber of commerce, the executive director of the local economic development council, civic leaders in the local Rotary/Kiwanis/America Legion/Lions/Elks, former elected officials, state legislator(s), and in many cases the publisher of the local weekly newspaper.

As you're researching to identify potential influencers, you're also scouting out what business and civic groups you may want to speak to, and share the reputation of your company and the merits of your project.

Investing in community due diligence can help you identify these key stakeholders. Additionally, you should also investigate the economic drivers that sustain the community financially. Is it tourism, farming, manufacturing, or something unique? For example, one project in a mid-western town, the landfill was the primary source of revenue.

OPPOSITION DUE DILIGENCE

Opposition due diligence, or in the political world we call it opposition research, you must cast a wide net. You begin by assessing neighboring homeowners and businesses to your project. Part of your research is to see if there have been any prior NIMBY-type conflicts involving your property or those nearby.

I would encourage you to also research any prior or current NIMBY opposition in other parts of the city or county. NIMBY forces may not be paying attention in your direction, but they may co-opt your project in the future, so it's worth noting to ensure no surprises.

If your property has a prior history of NIMBY conflicts, then you must dig deeper into what happened, who led it, who voted for and against the project, are there any elected officials still in office, is there a Facebook page, is it inactive, when was the last post, and if the project was approved, how is it doing?

At the very least, your due diligence will identify the leader or leaders of the opposition that may come after you down the road. Hence, the advantage you have created for yourself in this scenario: You know your opposition before they know you. This empowers you to proactively pre-empt and mediate anticipated accusations and attacks. This is operating from the strategic high ground based on the intel you gathered, vetted, and decided upon.

Sometimes when the intel is conflicting, you must jump into the fray to learn about the fate of your project sooner rather than later.

In the mid-2000s, I lost a very lucrative client who retained me for a year for an infill project, but the project ended after only 60 days. The client's attorney told the client that he had the majority votes at city hall, but they were not going to vote for the project until the homeowners near the project were won over.

The client told me the bankrupt golf course was surrounded by homeowners who didn't want to see it developed. My due diligence was finding conflicting intel that didn't make sense. There were indications that the community wanted to see the project get approved, but the city commissioners didn't.

So, we knocked on doors of what I called the "ring of fire". We quickly learned that two thirds of the homeowners wanted to see the project come in. In fact, one of the homeowners who supported the project, worked at city hall. She shared that not one commissioner or the mayor wanted the project.

This contradicted the information the attorney was giving the client. I went back and asked the client had he actually met with any of the elected officials, which he had not. I recommended that he meet with each official, which oddly, the lawyer counseled against.

I informed the client that there's support for the project, but intel gathered says the project is "dead on arrival" at city hall. Finally, the client followed my advice and met with each elected official, without the lawyer, and confirmed his project wasn't going get a single vote. As it turned out, the due diligence exposed the lawyer, who knew this truth for some time, but kept the client in the dark to keep the project and his billable hours going.

The client thanked me, fired the lawyer, and pulled the plug on the project.

POLITICAL DUE DILIGENCE

What's the primary purpose of any elected official regardless of office? It doesn't matter if they're the President, Senator, Congresswomen, State Legislator, Mayor, Councilman, or Township Clerk, everyone of these elected officials wants to get re-elected.

Your integrated public affairs strategy must account for upcoming elections, the primary dates and early voting, as well as knowing who is up for re-election, what seats are open, and who is going to run. Surprisingly, developers submit their applications in the heart of an election year, handing the opposition an early Christmas present – they now can make the project a high-profile campaign issue.

The sooner you get your arms around the voting records of the elected body, their tenure, their campaign issues, their contributors, their prior election victories, their positions on growth and development, and quotes in the news media, their campaign opponents, their posts on their campaign Facebook pages, the sooner you can decide on when to engage the community and whom you engage.

Of course, by retaining a local land-use lawyer and/or political consultant, you'll get their abridged knowledge, which is great, but you'll be surprised on how much more you'll learn by investing a few hours of online research going through the municipal website, reading minutes, agendas, public comments, emails, coupled with news articles, social media posts, and election results.

If you invest in additional due diligence, you may also discover existing alliances or feuds between elected officials, which can be crucial to securing a majority approval of the application. Moreover, you want to learn sooner than later how influential are planning boards and municipal staff such as the city manager, county administrator, or planning director.

In some cases, elected bodies rely heavily on boards and staff recommendations, while in other cases they go mostly ignored. This is where early due diligence, encapsulated in an integrated public affairs strategy pays dividends.

CORPORATE DUE DILIGENCE

Some of the greatest obstacles I've ever encountered in trying to defeat NIMBY forces came from within the corporate culture of the client. The culture ranges from being beholden to conventional thinking to hubris and ego to a bevy of corporate silos...or all the above.

When I first started out as a consultant in the early 2000s, I had a big box client ask me to set up a community meeting that expected over 200 local neighbors. The audience dynamics were encouraging – a 50/50 split for/against. The meeting was in the early stages, so the narrative was still early and non-threatening.

However, the corporate legal department of this big box retailer assigned a local lawyer to be the presenter, which was catastrophic. The lawyer lacked any emotional intelligence. He was condescending, terse, aggravated, and unlikable.

When a neighbor asked the lawyer a zoning question, he retorted, "That's a legal question and I'm not going to answering it." At that precise moment, the audience turned 100 percent against the project. There were three homeowner association presidents in the audience, all stood together and announced they were forging an alliance to oppose the project.

Two of the three HOA presidents were leaning towards supporting the project before the lawyer killed the community goodwill that the big-box community affairs team (who engaged me to help them) established before the meeting. Note: we were able to overcome the set back and the project was approved two years later.

One of the big giveaways of corporate silos are the comments, "We've never done that before" or "It's not in my job description."

Corporate due diligence is about identifying top/down opportunities and liabilities to achieve bottom/up success. You don't have to pursue a complete culture shift within an organization, but just enough due diligence to help associates feel empowered to ensure compliance and performance.

I've found a little encouragement, some cross training, and a positive team approach, quickly powers up any integrated public affairs operation full of accountability and success.

STRATEGIC PUBLIC AFFAIRS PLAN

By preparing a strategic public affairs plan, you're transitioning from a reactive, defensive model to a proactive, responsive campaign. The former is inductive and blind, while the latter is deductive, and lets you see the full chess board. When you map out a public affairs strategy, you're leveling up your citizen engagement game to higher levels of success.

Now that you're armed with due diligence intelligence, you can proceed to design a real time strategy. Here are elements to designing an effective strategic structure and plan:

Legal Critical Path: This is done mostly by the lawyers. In the strategy we need to put in the anticipated filing date and public hearing schedule, so we can plan before, during, and after the filing target date. The public affairs strategy protects the political flanks of the legal strategy.

Intelligence Report: Summarize the information and intelligence gathered from the due diligence protocols. Concisely spell out the opportunities to be pursued and the threats that need to be mitigated. This also includes profiling of the opposition that you discovered.

Messaging: Plug in the messaging that you developed on your company, your project, promotional facts, and mitigating answers to anticipated accusations. You should have your themes, core messaging and sub-messaging (supportive) points itemized and ready to be copied and pasted.

Benchmarks: In bullet point format, itemize out what you want to accomplish to track progress and be accountable. Targeting number of meetings, number of advocates recruited, opening a potential field office, development of project website, filing application, activating advocacy, developing marketing materials etc.

Timeline: Depending how far out you are from filing the application, breaking down project management objectives in monthly or weekly tasks to be accomplished.

Budget: Developing a proposed budget for producing brochures, one-pagers, producing and placing paid media (print/radio/Facebook), texting, social media outreach, video production, and other elements that may be necessary to move the needle forward. These are projections, but giving the team an idea ahead of time is the objective.

SITUATIONAL AWARENESS

In the military there's what they call the "fog of war", which means not everything will go as planned. There will be curveballs and unexpected twists and turns during the approval process. So, you must be flexible and ready to adapt and overcome these unexpected obstacles.

Fortunately, because you have a strategic plan with tactics mapped out, you can quickly, confidently, and rapidly respond to the chaotic environment. This is called situational awareness, which is an undervalued skillset that often determines the fate of the project.

CONTROLLING YOUR DESTINY

One of the greatest hoaxes perpetuated in the NIMBY Matrix™ it gives developers a false sense of control over the fate of their projects. This illusion is eventually shattered by the shock and awe of NIMBY attacks. I lost count how many times I've seen developers at public hearings or town hall meetings get blindsided, looking like a deer in the headlights before getting run over by the opposition.

If it wasn't such a sad sight to see, it would be funny. For those development professionals who have been red pilled and preparing their public affairs operations earlier in the process, there's a realistic sense of control and confidence over the fate of your project. The NIMBY Matrix™ is unable to hide its secrets or distract you away from low hanging fruit that's ready to be picked by the $A=CE^2$ formula for success.

There's only one thing left before this book is concluded and that's ensuring you have an A.C.E. Up Your Sleeve from the moment you finish this book to many years and projects down the road.

A.C.E. UP YOUR SLEEVE

The sad truth is some people will finish this book and ignore the wealth of knowledge, know-how, and community that's available to them. The good news is for those who venture forward, this book becomes a ticket to join an exclusive group of professionals and thought leaders focused on higher levels of success in securing the community-at-large's license to operate.

If you're interested in turning the words in *Breaking Out of the NIMBY Matrix™* into greater success, then keep on reading to learn how to get an A.C.E. up your sleeve.

Successful Leaders Do Not Settle for Second Best!

The NIMBY Matrix™ is responsible for countless defeats resulting in untold trillions of dollars in losses creating risks that no longer can be ignored. The good news is *Breaking Out of the NIMBY Matrix™* is very achievable, but you'll need more than a paradigm-shattering book to sustain success in the everchanging digital NIMBY world.

Unlike the good 'ole days where embarrassing defeats could be quickly swept under the rug, today's defeats are high-profile, Google-featured black eyes that's become too political, too public, and in today's digital NIMBY world, too costly for leaders who want to continue achieving their goals.

For too long, the public square has been dominated by digital NIMBY activists representing a very small sub-set of citizens willing to sacrifice the greater good of the community to advance their status quo agenda. They're on a mission to generate chaos, conflict, and celebrity, while alienating local decision makers. They claim to represent the "silent majority", but in reality, they're a very loud squeaky wheel getting the political grease.

Fortunately, there's a growing number of professionals who are tired of the unnecessary and disgraceful clashes in the public square.

It was my goal in writing this book to help corporate leaders, business professionals, and local officials see the NIMBY Matrix™ for what it is – a construct built on old paradigms that have instigated anti-development activism for decades. It's also my goal moving forward to empower leaders who want to turn their knowledge from this book into action that achieves greater accomplishments.

A.C.E. UP YOUR SLEEVE

In the NIMBY Matrix™ the public square is where sustainable real estate development projects have gone to die. What was once an inevitable defeat can now become an opportunity for those who want to lead in their fields.

I founded the Academy of Citizen Engagement (A.C.E.) to assemble and serve a select community of professional men and women who don't settle for second best. The Academy of Citizen Engagement caters to an exclusive membership serious about winning the "hearts and minds" of community stakeholders who grant the license to operate.

A.C.E. is an invitation-only organization offering programs and private services. Members receive VIP-level attention and a suite of services including high-quality continued online courses, master seminars, invitation-only webinars, one-on-one coaching, corporate training, as well as organizational assessments and project consultation.

Our A.C.E. members comprise of organizational leaders, corporate executives, real estate development professionals, government officials, and academics committed to improving upon their reputations for success in educating, empowering, and influencing the audiences that impact their bottom-line interests.

The majority of our members are mostly referred to by existing members. However, A.C.E. considers prospective members who sign up through our online waiting list. If you're interested in learning more about A.C.E. and potentially joining our elite society of professionals, then this book is an A.C.E. up your sleeve to begin the process of securing a competitive advantage in the NIMBY Matrix™.

Go to www.AceMyAudience.com and complete our preliminary membership application to join our waiting list. Because you've read this book, you get a special Select Screening Code: ACEBook When you use this code it will tell us that you have read the book, which will expedite the process.

Upon receiving your preliminary application and select screening code: ACEBook. An introductory call will be scheduled with me to discuss your expectations for success and our *A.C.E. Way of Excellence*.

I wish you well in your NIMBY Matrix™ journey. It's my sincere hope that our paths cross. I will be looking forward to scheduling our call in the near future.

Go to www.AceMyAudience.com and use your Select Screening Code: **ACEBook**

Best to You.

Patrick Slevin

P.S. If you have immediate questions about a project that is under fire or poised for application, you're welcomed to contact me to schedule a no-obligation exploratory call. My email is P.SL7@patrickslevin.com.

ACE
Academy of Citizen Engagement

ABOUT PATRICK SLEVIN

Corporate clients audaciously call him *NIMBY Whisperer.* Anti-development activists maliciously call him *NIMBY Slayer.* Real estate developers zealously call him to neutralize NIMBY opponents attacking their high-stakes sustainable projects. Over the span of his 25-year career, Patrick Slevin has established himself as an expert in the specialty of integrated public affairs, while earning a national reputation for his exceptional skills to rapidly turn NIMBY controversies into project approvals.

In 1996, Patrick Slevin was elected one of the youngest mayors in the country. At 27, he led the Tampa Bay city of Safety Harbor, Florida. As mayor in one the most urbanized counties in the nation, Slevin encountered and neutralized anti-development opposition before ever hearing of the infamous acronym NIMBY (Not-In-My-Backyard).

Today, Patrick Slevin is the Founder of the Academy of Citizen Engagement, Co-Founder of Citizens for Responsible

Government, and Past President of Network of Entrepreneurs & Business Advocates. He leads his integrated public affairs firm, SL7 Consulting, headquartered in Tallahassee, Florida.

Slevin is a two-time winner of the prestigious Public Relations Society of America's Silver Anvil Award of Excellence for Crisis & Issues Management. He has been featured in Influence Magazine as a "Great Communicator". Campaigns & Elections Magazine recognized Slevin as one of the nation's top political "Movers' & Shakers".

In 2021, Slevin published his first #1 Amazon bestselling book, Never Lose to NIMBY Opposition Again!: Master the Secrets, Strategies, and Solutions to Turn NIMBY Crisis Into Your Finest Hour, which became an instant success. It was the first NIMBY book published in decades empowering real estate development leaders with a "break glass in case of emergency" playbook to effectively turn crisis into success.

He is a highly sought speaker on the NIMBY subject matter. For nearly 20 years, Slevin has been a keynote, panelist, instructor, or moderator before real estate and business organizations from coast-to-coast including:

- Urban Land Institute (ULI)
- Commercial Real Estate Development Association (NAIOP)
- International Council of Shopping Centers (ICSC)
- Commercial Real Estate Women (CREW)
- Building Owners and Managers Association International (BOMA)

- American Planning Association (APA)
- Iowa Finance Authority
- Texas Housing Conference
- Tennessee Municipal League
- As well as homebuilders, biomass, energy, local chambers, economic development councils, municipalities, and corporate/not-for-profit board retreats.

Slevin studied *Organizational Leadership* at Eckerd College in St. Petersburg, Florida. His business coursework included Principles of Leadership, Organizational Behavior & Leadership, Technology & Society, Complex Organizations, Managing Cultural Diversity, Work & Occupations, Evaluation Research Methods, Organizational Dynamics, Public Administration, Organizational Consultation, and Political Organizations.

He completed the MIT-Harvard Public Disputes Program *Dealing with an Angry Public*, sponsored by Harvard Law School in 2004.

Slevin is a veteran of the United States Air Force, where he honorably served in the security forces from 1988 to 1996 for both active duty and ready reserve.

Patrick Slevin resides in Tallahassee, Florida with his wife Sharon where they enjoy their two young grandsons Easton and Logan.

CONTRIBUTING CHAPTER CO-AUTHORS

Any good integrated public affairs consultant should present themselves as a public affairs generalist with many specialties. Over the years, I've excelled in crisis management, grassroots advocacy, stakeholder engagement, corporate communications, public relations, campaign management, political marketing, alliance development, and professional speaking.

However, there are three areas where I collaborate with experts in their respective fields of legal, digital, and video. You cannot successfully defeat NIMBY opposition in today's digital NIMBY world without these crucial disciplines operating within an integrated public affairs toolbox.

I'm proud and thankful to be collaborating on three chapters with the best in the business.

CHAPTER 11: LEVELING UP YOUR LEGAL GAME

Land Use Lawyer: Brian Seymour, Esq.

Brian Seymour, Esq. co-chairs the real property practice of the Gunster Law Firm, with thirteen offices located throughout Florida. Operating from his West Palm Beach office, Brian is one of the go-to real estate and environmental lawyers for new development, redevelopment, and land use and zoning changes, often brought into the most impactful, complex, and often controversial development projects.

I asked Brian to be a co-chapter contributor because he is one of the best lawyers in the business and we've collaborated on behalf of our mutual clients and many NIMBY projects.

Brian shares his legal insights in our chapter titled, *Leveling Up Your Legal Game*. Of course, Brian isn't giving legal advice, but rather, sharing his insights on how he leverages his legal acumen in the NIMBY Matrix™.

CHAPTER 12: DIGITAL AWARENESS IN A NIMBY WORLD

Digital Marketing Expert: Jennings DePriest

Jennings Lawton DePriest I is CEO and Founder of Top Lobster, a boutique digital influence advisory firm. Jennings is one of the only professionals on earth with experience as a lobbyist, chief marketing officer, and political campaign strategist.

He is also the author of Bottom Line Politics: How Your Business Can Fight the Government–and Win, and contributing guest author to the Amazon bestselling book, Breaking Out of the NIMBY Matrix: Red Pill Success in a Digital NIMBY World.

Jennings alters public opinion to take clients from submissive and fearful to dominant and influential. Learn more at www.jenningsdepriest.com.

CHAPTER 13: LIGHTS, CAMERA, ACTION

Video Producer and Film Director: Charles Belvin

I've been working with Charlie Belvin for over a decade. Every year that has gone by, I've engaged his services more and more – due to the increasing influence of video communications. I'm thankful to have crossed paths with this four-time Emmy award winning video communications master. The bottom line, you cannot tell your story, convey your narrative, or execute persuasive impressions without including video in your public affairs toolkit.

In our chapter, *Lights, Camera, Action*, Charlie shares his gifted insights on the power of video communications, and why it's a go-to for any real estate development project. Real estate development can be very impersonal and easy to demonize. However, video communications can effectively humanize an otherwise lifeless site plan, zoning or permitting application.

ACKNOWLEDGEMENTS

I could not have written this book without the countless hours of researching, writing, speaking, counseling, operating, and studying the human condition. Every project and campaign has successes, misfires, and occasional failures, and the people I've worked alongside have left their impressions upon me.

I'm very thankful for the Forward provided by Pat Moore and the three co-authored chapters provided by Brian, Jennings, and Charlie. I would like to thank Evelio Silvera, who helped get my first book published as well as this latest book – both Amazon bestsellers.

A lot of my public affairs work is outside of the spotlight and thrives on confidentiality. I cannot name those clients and even colleagues who have entrusted me with their companies, reputations, and projects. In many cases, we've become friends and remain in touch despite the years and distance. You know who you are and I'm thankful we fought in the trenches and shared many victories.

My wife Sharon did the editing duties and not only found missing words and other basic editing help, but offered terrific guidance on improving the book. She wanted me to share more of my war stories, which so I did. Thank you for leveling up the book for others to enjoy.

Lastly, I want to thank those who are not only reading this book, but choosing to take the red pill. You will learn not only how to succeed in the NIMBY Matrix™, but become the 1 % of elite professionals for others to follow. You will gain insights that many won't be able to perceive or understand, so it's up to you, if you want to help others see the true realities of the NIMBY Matrix™.

I hope you choose to pay it forward – maybe not with your competitors.

Made in the USA
Middletown, DE
28 October 2024